Transcripts Made Easy

The Homeschooler's Guide to
High School Paperwork

Janice Campbell

Everyday Education
Making time for things that matter.
www.EverydayEducation.com • www.DoingWhatMatters.com

Transcripts Made Easy

Everyday Education, LLC

P. O. Box 549

Ashland, VA 23005

Everyday-Education.com

TranscriptsMadeEasy.com

Edition 4 © 2018 Everyday Education, LLC

Cover images (top to bottom): © Seanlockephotography | Dreamstime.com, © Wong Sze Yuen | Dreamstime.com, © Photographerlondon | Dreamstime.com.

ISBN-13: 978-1-61322-048-1

Campbell, Janice

Transcripts made easy: the homeschooler's guide to high school paperwork / Janice Campbell

1. Education—Home Schooling. 2. Education—Reference. 3. Reference—Handbooks & Manuals. I. Title.

Standard Legal Disclaimer

The information in this book is intended to provide general record-keeping and transcript information for homeschool parents, and does not constitute legal advice or supersede the laws of your state. Because homeschool laws change fairly often, it is important to keep up with applicable regulations, and to comply with them.

Contents

Part 4

Part 5

Part 6

To all the homeschooling moms and dads—

your dedication and love are an inspiration to me.

May you be blessed throughout this journey.

Janice

The supreme end of education is expert discernment in all things—

the power to tell the good from the bad,

the genuine from the counterfeit,

and to prefer the good and the genuine

to the bad and the counterfeit.

Samuel Johnson

Preface

Dear Friends,

So it's time to think about high school! I hope you are excited about that because it is one of the most interesting stages of homeschooling. There are so many wonderful things your teen can do! With a little planning and simple record-keeping, high school can be a great time to get a jump start on college, explore potential careers through an internship or microbusiness, learn through travel, and more.

Whatever your student does for high school, you will need to keep records. Even if you are a relaxed homeschooler or an unschooler, your teen will eventually need a transcript. Since I am sure you would rather spend your time on people, rather than paperwork, I created *Transcripts Made Easy* to make planning, record-keeping, and transcript-making easy. In it, you will find a complete system for keeping simple records and making a transcript that highlights your student's strengths and achievements. You can use as much or as little of the system as you please, and you will not even have to buy or learn to use special software.

Because you are not just teaching—you are doing the work of a guidance counselor as well, this new edition of *Transcripts Made Easy* has been updated with more information to help you feel confident with your homeschool paperwork. Many people who used earlier editions have asked good questions, so you will find many of the answers to those questions woven through the text. In addition, I have reorganized everything to follow the flow of the transcript planning process so it will be easier to pick up and go to exactly the section you need. For a couple of important special topics, I have asked guest experts to share their best tips. Each expert has offered guidance in an area in which she has extensive experience, and each has a book or website which can provide more answers in these areas.

- Professor Carol Reynolds, longtime college professor and author of *Why Freshmen Fail,* has shared seven tips on how to prepare your student for success in the first year of college.

- Judith Munday, a professional special-needs consultant who also contributed to the previous edition, has updated the information in the chapter on creating transcripts for special-needs students.

- Kathy Kuhl, author of *Homeschooling the Struggling Learner* has shared some excellent resource suggestions for learning about timing and testing requirements for special-needs accommodations.

- And while it is not a guest expert, the free GPA calculator at our website can help you quickly, easily, and accurately figure a grade point average for your student's transcript. (FreeGPACalc.com)

Whatever your situation, whether you are following a traditional high school course of study or are doing unusual and exciting things, you will find what you need to know about record-keeping and transcripts in these pages. If you have a question that you do not see addressed, please e-mail me at janice@doingwhatmatters.com. I will do my best to help.

I wish you joy as you homeschool through high school!

Janice Campbell

Ashland, Virginia

2001; 2007; 2010; 2018

Meet the Transcript

What is a transcript?

A transcript is a record of what a student has studied. A high school transcript covers the courses required to earn a high school diploma. A transcript is not a portfolio that would contain samples of student work and other proofs of accomplishment. Rather, it is a concise overview, like a résumé. It can be seen as a snapshot of a student's intellectual foundation, and as a passport into the next stage of life.

Who needs a transcript?

Every high school student should have a transcript. First, it is an important record of the student's education. Even if the student does not plan to go to college at the time of graduation, a transcript should be created, because plans change. An employer may require an employee to take a course, or the student may want to change careers or join the military at some point. Some car insurance companies grant discounts based on a student's high school transcript. Since the transcript is one of the standard requirements for entrance to many future opportunities, it is one of the most important pieces of paperwork you will create for your student.

Who will see the transcript?

Like a résumé, the transcript is designed to provide information to the gatekeepers of opportunity. College admissions counselors, scholarship committees, military recruiters, trade school admissions personnel, and possibly even potential employers will see the transcript whenever the student seeks admission to a program, job, or class. As the student gains higher education credentials, the high school transcript will be less used, but in the first few years after high school, it can be a passport to new opportunities.

What are the parts of the transcript?

There are three major sections on every transcript: the Identity section, Basic Information section, and Course Record section. Here is an overview of what each part contains, followed by a detailed breakdown of what goes where:

1. **Identity**: This section of the transcript identifies the document, the student, the school, and the date of graduation.

2. **Basic Information**: In this part of the transcript, you will define a grading scale, the number of hours that equals a unit, and the abbreviations used for credit by exam or dual-credit classes. If you are an unschooler who does not use grades, a brief statement of your non-grading philosophy would replace the grading scale. The signature of the certifying parent can appear in this section as well.

3. **Course Record**: This is the body of the transcript—a final record of all the courses your student has completed during the high school years, along with grades and credits earned.

Here is a detailed look at what each section contains and why.

Part One: Identity

The first section of the transcript identifies the document (a transcript), the school that is issuing the transcript, and the student whose education is the subject of the transcript. The first item is a title which identifies the document. You may list it in a variety of ways:

- High School Transcript
- Official Homeschool Transcript
- Private School Transcript

- Transcript
- Stagg Creek High School Transcript (school name plus "Transcript")

There is no right, one-size-fits-all title, just as there is no one-size-fits-all homeschool. Choose the title you prefer, and use it with confidence.

Student Information

This section provides information about the student's identity while he or she was in high school. If, for example, you are a bit late in getting the transcript created, and your daughter has married, you will still put her maiden name on the transcript because that is the name she used while in high school.

Student's Name: Use the student's full legal name, including first, middle, and last names. It is your decision whether to list it in filing order (last name first) or first name first. You will see it both ways on the samples.

Date of Birth: Use numerals for this, usually MM/DD/YYYY.

Social Security Number (SSN): This is optional, and I do not recommend putting it on the transcript. The school to which your student applies will need the SSN for their records, but it will be requested with other paperwork. Since high school transcripts are sometimes submitted with scholarship applications, it is best to keep the SSN off the transcript in order to limit the possibility of misuse.

Sex/Gender: Optional, but recommended if the student's name is not gender-specific (Leslie, Tyler, Beverly).

Parents: This is another optional line, but may be helpful if your signatures are illegible. If you choose to list your names, list them in legal format (Henry R. and Katherine T. Ford) rather than social format (Mr. and Mrs. Hank Ford).

Admission Date: Sometimes optional. Also referred to as "Date of Entry," this is just the date when your student started high school. If your student began high school work in some subjects early, so that a start date would make it appear as if high school had taken more than four years, I suggest not including this date unless a particular college requests it. If you do include it, use the MM/DD/YYYY format.

Graduation Date: The date when the student completed the required number of credits for high school graduation. Use the same format as the Admission Date. If you are sending a transcript while the student is still in high school, list this as the "Anticipated Graduation Date."

Grade Point Average: A final grade point average can appear in this section or in the Course Record section, depending on the transcript format you choose.

School Information

If you have not decided on a name for your school before now, you can make a quick decision, or you can just choose to identify your school as "Homeschool." There is no legal requirement to influence your decision, so it can be whatever you prefer.

School Name: This is what you call your own homeschool. Do not use the name of your curriculum provider (e.g., Memoria Press High School), any name that could be confused with a public high school in your area, or any other name that would imply connection with an official organization (e.g., Virginia SOL Academy). You may use:

- Your last name (Hernandez High School)
- Your street name (Connor Avenue Prep School)
- A local geographic feature (Stagg Creek High School; Mount Wilson Family School)
- A descriptive name (Great Books Academy; Discovery Classical High School)
- A religious name (Living Word Homeschool; St. Joseph Homeschool)

You may select anything that you feel effectively describes your school and does not infringe upon the identity of another institution.

School Address: This is the only address information that appears on the transcript, because transcripts are requested from schools, not from students. This is because students are assumed to have moved on in life, while schools usually remain in the same place.

Telephone Number: Optional. This is usually included on the application so does not necessarily have to be included with the transcript.

E-mail: Optional, but can be useful. If you choose to include an email, it is best if it sounds reasonably serious and grown up. Pumpkinhead@email.com just does not sound quite like an adult!

Previous School: If the student began high school enrolled in a public or private school, list the name and address here. The transcript you issue will cover only the years you actually taught your student, so the college you choose will also need official transcripts from any other schools attended.

This is the end of the Identity section (you will notice that the explanation was a lot longer than the actual section!). However you design your document, this section will usually be at the top of the page for easy filing. Be sure each element is easy to find and identify, as in the sample transcripts later in this book.

Part Two: Basic Information

This section includes essential information that will help clarify the meaning of different elements within the Course Record. Depending on the transcript format, this section will usually contain:

- A grading scale or non-grading philosophy
- The number of hours that equals a unit
- Key to abbreviations used to identify classes taken through a co-op or other school, dual-credit classes, honors classes, etc.
- Space for the signature of the certifying parent or parents

In order to fill out this section, you will refer to the detailed information in the Grading section of this book, along with your state's homeschool law or requirements.

Part Three: Course Record

Although this section has the shortest description, it represents the longest part of the transcript. The Course Record provides an overview of all the classes taken in high school. To fill out this section, you will condense the information from Class Profiles and Subject Worksheets into a concise list of courses, grades, credit granted, and grade point averages. You will find complete instructions for this in the remainder of this book.

Overview of the Transcript Process

Before beginning the transcript

- Learn what a transcript is and what goes on it (Part 1).
- Make a plan that covers the basics and fits your student (Part 2).
- Learn how to document for special needs or circumstances (Part 3).
- Set up a simple record-keeping system (Part 3):
  - *pocket folder*
  - *high school binder*
  - *class profiles*
  - *subject worksheets*
  - *student record booklet*
  - *reading log*

While teaching

- Continue to cultivate skills and habits needed for adulthood (Part 2).
- Help your student prepare for college or vocation (Part 2).
- Have a record-keeping routine (Part 3).
  - *Keep student work samples.*
  - *Plan with Class Profiles.*
  - *Use Subject Worksheets and Logs as needed.*
  - *Record classes in student record booklet when complete.*

Before the end of the first year

- Create a blank transcript to fill in (Part 5).
  - *Add courses at the beginning of the school year.*
- Grade each course (Part 4)
- Grant credit, measured in Carnegie Units (Part 4).
- Calculate the semester and cumulative GPA (Part 4).
  - *Add grades and credit to the transcript form at the end of each year.*

When applying for college and preparing for graduation

- Print official copies of the transcript (Part 5).
- Create diploma (Part 5).

Where to Start in This Book

Welcome to the world of high school record-keeping! *Transcripts Made Easy* is designed so that you can jump in at any point and use only the parts you need. Here are some suggestions to help you decide where to start.

If You Just Want to Learn About Planning

You do not have to be homeschooling a teen in order to be interested in learning how to keep good records. No matter what age your student is, it is probably not too early to begin thinking about how to keep student work and create simple records. You will probably find what you need in parts two and three: Plan With the End in Mind and Keep Simple Records. There are also some helpful resources in part six: References, Resources, and Reproducibles.

If Your Student is in Junior High School

You are in the right place! Read through this book; choose the ideas that best suit your teaching style, and begin keeping records with the first high school-level class your student takes. It is that easy!

If Your Student is in the First Two Years of High School

You probably already know what you are doing for academics, so just skim through the introduction to high school, and jump into the record-keeping ideas. If you have not been keeping records, start to catch up now. If you have records of some sort, start a transcript form, and fill in as many semesters as you have completed. For the rest of high school, you may decide to use the Subject Worksheets or just continue with what you have been using. Either way, if you keep the transcript current by filling in each semester as you complete it, you can relax and know that you have the paperwork under control.

If Your Student is a Junior

You are getting close to college application time! If you have kept records of any kind, it is time to start a transcript. Just choose a transcript format, follow the instruction in the "Create the Transcript Document" chapter to set it up on your computer, and start filling it in. If you do not have many records, you can jog your memory by using the Check-Off Transcript form to remind you of the basic subject categories you need to fill in. As an alternative, you may start by using Subject Worksheets to organize what you can remember. Be sure to read about "Skills and Habits to Cultivate in High School" and Professor Carol's "Seven Strategies for a Successful First Year at College." These are both found in Part 2, Plan with the End in Mind.

If Your Student is a Senior

You may feel that you are too late to get going, but do not worry; you can do it! You will follow the same procedure as the parent of a junior—you will just have to work faster. If you cannot remember all that your student has studied, just ask—he or she may be able to help you.

If You Need a Transcript Tomorrow

You do not have time to worry about details. Go directly to the Check-Off Transcript and fill in the Basic Information and Identity sections. Check off each subject your student has completed. Add as many grades as possible—grades from outside sources, grades based on AP, SAT II, or CLEP exams, and grades you remember. If you have grades for all classes, you can follow the instructions in the section on grading and granting credit, but if you have grades for only some classes, include those you have and just check off classes with no grades. The college admissions department will at least see the scope of what your student has covered and will be able to evaluate his abilities through standardized test scores.

Part 2

Plan with the End in Mind

What is the purpose of high school? How does it differ from the eight years of school you have already completed with your student? Just as teenagers are different from toddlers, high school is different from the years that have gone before. There are several areas of change:

- Level of difficulty in school subjects
- Level of student independence
- Increased options for outside study
- Increased responsibility for keeping records

As you think about high school, remember that it is still an education and not a rat race. There is quite a bit to cover and a few deadlines to meet, but if it is approached in a simple, orderly way, the student should have time to study and do the things that will equip him or her for the future. Having a positive high school experience begins with planning, and the best sort of planning begins with a vision for the future.

Plan with a Destination in Mind

What do you want to be when you grow up? It is a question that children are asked from the time they can talk, and often the answer is fanciful or off-hand. As a student nears the teen years, though, that question gets a bit more serious. What kind of future does your student envision, and how can you best help to prepare for it?

A good education begins with a solid foundation in core subjects and foundational skills, and is personalized with focused electives that relate to the student's abilities, interests, and goals. As you prepare to homeschool high school, you have a chance to create an educational experience that not only sparks a lifelong interest in study, but also:

- Fits the student's aptitudes, interests, and goals
- Cultivates cultural literacy and an interest in many subjects
- Encourages positive, healthy habits of mind, spirit, and body
- Becomes increasingly self-directed
- Meets or exceeds the requirements of law
- Meets or exceeds the requirements for entrance to the college or vocation of the student's choice
- Provides opportunities to acquire practical skills
- Prepares the student for life as an adult

Each experience and high school subject helps to prepare for the future, so your high school plans must be based on a vision of what the future holds for your student. Personality and career testing can help a student discern a future path (the Myers-Briggs Personality Type is a good place to start—myersbriggs.org). But first, foundational knowledge and basic skills must be established.

What to Study in High School

"Education should have two objects: first, to give definite knowledge, reading and writing, language and mathematics, and so on; secondly, to create those mental habits which will enable people to acquire knowledge and form sound judgments for themselves." Bertrand Russell, 1872–1970

A student who graduates from high school is expected to have a solid foundation in the communication, thinking, and numerical skills—reading, writing, speaking, logic, and mathematics. In addition he or she should have studied

- History, encompassing all aspects of individual civilizations up to and including the present, with attention to politics, religion, science, and the arts.
- Art and Music, including theory, appreciation, history, and applied experience.
- Science, including the history and application of scientific ideas and theories.

In most states, these disciplines can be covered using materials of your choice. This means that you may opt for a well-rounded living books curriculum such as the one outlined at Ambleside-

Online.org, classical education, faith-based materials, online courses, traditional textbooks, or any combination of methods. Some states offer reimbursement for curriculum purchases through a charter school umbrella, as long as the curriculum is of a non-sectarian nature.

Once you have a curriculum, you are responsible for following your state's homeschool law for record-keeping and testing. Beyond that, you will want to meet the admission standards for the most competitive future option that your student may be considering. If you have a budding physicist who wants to attend MIT, check the MIT website to find out how many years and what specific courses of math and science are required. If your student is a gifted musician and has his or her heart set on Peabody Conservatory, visit the school's website to discover what types of learning, performance experiences, and documentation must be accumulated. If you have a student athlete who wants to seek NCAA eligibility, visit the NCAA.org website early so that the high school experience and the transcript you create can help to achieve that goal.

The more selective the program or school, the more competitive the entrance requirements, so it is important to know what is necessary so you can cover it in the allotted time. Even if your student does not end up choosing one of the most selective options, shooting for higher requirements can provide excellent preparation for other schools considered.

Credits Needed

A college-bound student usually needs only sixteen core credits (also known as Carnegie units) and eight elective credits, for twenty-four total units. Students who are not college bound need even fewer—twenty-two units—thirteen core classes and nine electives. A two-semester class earns one Carnegie unit (you will learn more about this in the section on Grades, Credits, and the GPA), so the twenty-four-unit requirement can be broken down to four years of high school, six classes per year if you use a traditional schedule. That is not too bad, is it? On the next page, you will see a table that shows an average of how many credits are needed per subject.

College Alternative Requirements

Not all students go to a traditional four-year college right after high school. Some take a gap year for work, travel, missions, trade school, an apprenticeship, or just to gain a clearer idea of what they might want to do in life. Some students never go to college or postpone it for years, choosing instead to work in a trade, join the military, or pursue entrepreneurship. If you believe that your student may choose a college alternative, it is important to help them prepare to meet the entrance requirements of whatever path they have chosen. The College Alternatives chapter will point you toward resources that will help you discover what is needed for those paths.

Sample High School Requirements

Here is a fairly standard example of how many years or units states traditionally require for each basic subject in order to earn a high school diploma. Homeschoolers may not be subject to exactly the same guidelines, so be sure to check the homeschool law for your state. Also, remember that selective colleges will most likely have higher standards and more specific requirements, so those standards will be the most important ones to consider.

High school Graduation Requirements	Standard Diploma (General Ed.)	Advanced Diploma (College Prep)
English, including Literature	4	4
Math (All but one unit must be Algebra I or above)	3	4
Science (options include Earth Science, Biology, Chemistry, Physics)	3	4
History/Social Science	3	4
Foreign Language		3
Health/Physical Education	2	2
Fine Arts/Practical Arts	1	1
Electives	6	2
Total Units Needed	22	24
The Education Commission of the States offers an overview of specific state guidelines: www.ecs.org/high-school-graduation-requirements/ *The NCAA has specific requirements for student athletes:* www.ncaa.org/student-athletes/future/home-school-students		

Skills and Habits to Cultivate in High School

No matter what kind of future your students envision, high school is the time to be sure they have the basic skills they will need in college, trades, or the workforce. They will need to be able to communicate clearly in both speech and writing, and they will also need time management, organization, research, citation, and test-taking skills.

Communication Skills

High school is an ideal time to practice speech and composition skills, including timed and untimed essays and report writing, with appropriate research and correctly formatted citations. A writer's handbook such as *Write for College* (by Patrick Sebranek, et al.) or my own Excellence in Literature *Handbook for Writers* (writers-handbook.com) provides instructions for researching, writing, revising, and proofreading various types of essays, as well as help in developing the skills listed below.

Writing Basics Your Student Needs to Know

- How to write formal letters, essays, and research papers
- How to use a writer's handbook for reference and self-evaluation
- How to research using credible sources
- How to correctly format citations

Citations

I recommend that students learn to use at least one or two common citation methods for citing references in essay and report writing.

- MLA (Modern Language Association): This method of in-text citations seems to be most often used in literature and other humanities classes. It is a simple and logical method of citation, and it works well for many purposes. (style.mla.org)
- APA (American Psychological Association): This method of in-text citation was designed for use within the social and behavioral sciences. (apastyle.org)

- *Chicago Manual of Style*: This advanced, formal citation system uses footnotes and endnotes, and is often used for longer writing projects in history and humanities classes. (chicagomanualofstyle.org)

The Online Writing Lab (OWL) at Purdue University offers a comparison chart that gives a concise overview of each citation style and how it is used. (owl.english.purdue.edu/owl/resource/949/01/)

Online Research

Students must learn to conduct specific searches, select credible sources, and correctly cite information used. Online research can save astonishing amounts of time and money, but like traditional research, it can be done badly. Even though research seems easier with Internet access, it is still necessary to check facts and avoid plagiarism. Students must know that it is never okay to just copy and paste information found online. (style.mla.org/plagiarism-and-academic-dishonesty)

Reliable Research Resources

Remember fake news? In order to write good essays and reports, it is necessary to avoid the academic equivalent of fake news—unreliable sources. No source is perfect, but some sources are far more reliable than others. You are usually on steady ground with the information sources listed below.

- Scholarly books
- Academic databases offered through the local or college library
- Encyclopedia sites such as Encyclopedia Britannica
- Sites hosted by colleges (URL ends in .edu)

Wikipedia is a popular encyclopedia site that is user edited. That means that anyone, including you or me or your student can sign up and change the information in it. This makes it somewhat less reliable than other encyclopedias, but it can still be useful as a quick reference or a research starter. Just remind students to verify information with another source.

Personal Organization

Students need to know how to organize class information and paperwork. A three-ring binder is a classic way to organize all the material for a semester. It can hold a class profile or syllabus, assignment schedule, plus copies of all notes and written assignments. On the computer, it is helpful for the student to organize all work in a desktop folder labeled with name and semester (e.g.

Joy Last—Spring 2028). Inside the folder should be a sub-folder for each class, and in every class folder should be all the assignments from the class. Each assignment should be labeled with the class and assignment name. I recommend keeping all assignment files on the computer until the student graduates. If a student learns to keep everything together and organized while at home, getting assignments in on time at college will seem easier.

Time Management

A student who is old enough to do high school work is old enough to plan time wisely. One basic academic planning skill is learning to look at project due dates and create intermediate deadlines for each step. For example, if a student has four weeks in which to study a book and write papers, it is helpful to divide the number of pages by the study days available so that the book will be finished in time to do the writing assignments. Careful planning can prevent last minute cramming or hasty, ill-conceived papers. If the student needs extra help with time-management skills, Sean Covey's *The 7 Habits of Highly Effective Teens* or Julie Morgenstern's *Time Management from the Inside Out* can be very helpful.

Test-Taking Skills

There are simple test-taking techniques that will increase chances for success on a standardized test, but because homeschoolers typically do not spend a lot of time testing, they may need to practice the skills separately. The skills include knowing how to manage the limited time in a test, understanding the best way to approach multiple-choice questions, having a game plan for timed essays, and understanding the scoring system for the particular test. The test preparation books published by Princeton Review usually have excellent test-taking tips.

Before taking any of the major high school standardized tests, have the student take one or more sample exams from a test-prep book. That way, there will be few surprises and he or she will feel much more confident when taking the real thing. For sample tests, I suggest using the test-prep books published by the company that publishes the actual exams. The sample problems they offer seem to be most like the questions on the tests.

Scheduling Courses

When was the last time you thought about the best way to schedule your school days? Six subjects, one hour each per day, five days a week — ho hum. Maybe it is time to ask some questions about scheduling!

- Is an hour enough time for a student to read, grow interested in a subject, hear a lesson, and do the associated work?
- Does this format work equally well for all subjects?
- Is this the best format for your student's learning style?

Block scheduling or the one subject plan can allow time for students to immerse in a topic and get some serious work done. By the time students reach high school age, their brains are sufficiently well developed that they can easily skip a day, especially in subjects they enjoy, without forgetting material between days. The one-hour schedule, on the other hand, can be frustratingly short for subjects that would benefit from a longer period of concentration or practice.

Schedule Options to Consider

Fortunately, you can choose the type of scheduling that best fits your student and your lifestyle. The four years of school and six subjects per year, one hour per day schedule is easy to use, but there are other options that can help you teach some subjects more effectively. In fact, by the last couple years of school, it can be a good idea to present lessons one week at a time, allowing students to decide when and where to do the work. It is excellent preparation for managing time in college! Here are some possible schedule alternatives to consider.

College-Style Schedule

Study one group of subjects such as the humanities (history, literature, theology, philosophy, and the arts) on Monday and Wednesday, and math and the sciences on Tuesday and Thursday, spending two or more hours per day per subject. Use Friday as a study day to complete any leftover work or for field trips and errands.

Sequential Scheduling

Study one subject at a time, full time. As we will discuss in "How to Grant Credit," a year of study can be measured as 120 hours or the time it takes to cover a standard textbook. A highly motivated teen could work through one textbook per month by studying about six hours a day, five days a week and could theoretically complete high school in 22 to 24 months. Alternatively, it would be possible to study two subjects at a time, three hours per day each, and finish in the same amount of time. The best and deepest learning does not usually come from a textbook, so I would not use this for every subject, but it may be appropriate for a few courses.

One-Subject Plan

A similar option is what a nearby military academy calls the "One Subject Plan." The school year is divided into five seven-week terms, and during each term the students study only language arts and math plus one other subject. This intensely focused immersion style of learning is what our family used for independent or deadline-focused learning. It is especially useful if you are preparing for a major trip and want to do an in-depth study of the history, culture, and language of your destination. I have also used it for academic, business, and home-centered subjects, and the boys have used it to learn about subjects ranging from World War II to classical music, computer programming, HVAC, and novel-writing.

Year-Round Schooling

Year-round schooling is another scheduling option that works well for many families. They choose to school for ten weeks on, three weeks off, or two hours a day Monday through Thursday, or some other variation. Year-round schooling adapts well to frequent travel or other unusual situations, and can help families keep a regular routine going all year, rather letting it all go for three months and having start fresh each fall.

Sabbath Scheduling

Inspired by the idea of the sabbath—one day off after every six days of work—some homeschoolers do six weeks of school and take one week off, creating a one-week sabbath from school all through the year. The week off is a time when you can assess what is working and what is not, take special field trips, do creative projects, or just enjoy being off. This may be the most sensible idea of all!

Clustering

A related idea is to group similar subjects together so that linked knowledge is gained at the same time, boosting retention. For my sons, I grouped Western Civilization, British and World literature, art history, and music appreciation into a two year in-depth study, followed by one year of American history, government, art, and literature. Science and math can be grouped in similar ways.

One Way of Mixing Schedule Types

When we were doing school with the boys, we followed Charlotte Mason's advice and did short, focused lessons that gradually increased in length as they grew older. By high school, we found that daily short lessons were still most effective for problem-based subjects such as math, but a college- or block-style schedule was often more interesting and effective for classes in the humanities and sciences. For much of high school, we did math daily and focused on the humanities on Monday and Wednesday; the sciences, including labs, on Tuesday and Thursday. This balance seemed to work effectively for all of us, and was a good preparation for the longer classes they encountered in college.

Sample Four-Year Schedule for College-Bound Students

Here is an overview of the approximate timing for classes, tests, and applications in an average high school schedule. Remember to base your student's high school courses and schedule on the most selective option that the teen may consider.

	Course Plan	Tests to Take	Applications to Send	Skills to Develop	Other Suggestions
Year 1	• 6 classes per semester • 1 unit of each core subject	• Personality and aptitude profile (MBTI or other) • 16personalities.com		• Independent time management • Annotate books and take good notes	• Read widely • Record books in a reading log (every year) • Begin considering career aptitudes
Year 2	• 6 classes per semester • 1 unit of each core subject			• Practice test-taking skills and timed essay writing	• Begin researching colleges/alternatives • Consider a local or virtual college tour
Year 3	• 6 classes per semester • Core subjects plus electives	• Fall: PSAT • Spring: SAT, ACT, or CLT	• May/June: Begin sending college applications	• More independent time management; advanced essay writing	• Narrow college and career options (see college comparison information below) • Visit colleges during spring break if desired
Year 4	• Equivalent of 6 classes per semester • Core subjects plus electives	• SAT II, AP, or CLEP as required • Retake SAT/ACT if desired	• Apply for financial aid at FAFSA.ed.gov, and individual scholarships as needed	• Continue to practice and maintain all skills, with increasingly independent time management	• Register for scholarship search engines such as • Scholarships.com • Fastweb.com
Student athletes seeking NCAA eligibility should consult NCAA guidelines for specific information. www.ncaa.org/student-athletes/future/home-school-students					
College Comparison Sites collegescorecard.ed.gov cardinalnewmansociety.org www.niche.com/colleges/search/best-christian-colleges			The Common Application or the Universal College Application can be used for many colleges: commonapp.org www.universalcollegeapp.com		

Standardized Tests to Consider

Students may take a number of standardized tests in high school. While each type of exam consists primarily of multiple-choice questions, the exams are designed to measure different things. You can take exams to gain entrance to a college, to add credibility to your transcript grades, or to get a head start on college (my book, *Get a Jump Start On College,* has more information on how to do this). Some of these exams may be taken at any time during high school, but others need to be taken during a specific year.

Aptitude Tests

The most commonly taken exams—the Preliminary Scholastic Aptitude Test (PSAT), the Scholastic Aptitude Test (SAT), and the ACT (formerly American College Testing)—measure aptitude and readiness for college-level work in language arts and math. One or more of these exams are usually required for college admissions.

- The PSAT, usually taken in eleventh grade, is not necessary for college admission, but it can be good practice for the SAT, and taking it then allows students to compete for a National Merit Scholarship. (collegeboard.com)

- The SAT: A general exam that tests verbal and math skills. It is often used for admission. The SAT is a 3-hour test, mostly multiple choice. This test changes periodically, so be sure to get a current SAT study guide. (collegeboard.com)

- ACT: An alternate general exam often used for admission. The ACT tests English, Math, Reading, and Science Reasoning. About 3 hours, all multiple choice. (act.org)

- CLT: The Classic Learning Test is a unique alternative to the ACT or SAT. It measures academic formation, accomplishment, and potential. According to the designers o the exam, "The Classic Learning Test (CLT) invites students to wrestle with works of the greatest minds in history across literary and mathematical content. Rich material reflecting both theistic and secular perspectives benefits and enriches the student in the test-taking process." (cltexam.com)

Knowledge and Achievement Tests

A second group of exams, including Advanced Placement (AP) and SAT II exams, evaluates knowledge in specific subjects in order to grant advanced placement in college. A third group of exams, which includes CLEP and DSST, tests subject knowledge in order to grant college credit. The AP and SAT II exams are administered through high schools, while the CLEP and DSST exams are administered through colleges.

- AP: Subject-area tests for advanced-level knowledge. Many colleges grant advanced placement or college credit for a score of 3 or greater. (collegeboard.com)
- SAT II: Subject-area tests (22 subjects available) that are used either for admissions or placement, depending on college policy. One hour, mostly multiple choice. (collegeboard.com)
- CLEP: Subject-area exams. Many colleges grant 3-6 credits or advanced placement for a passing score. This is a 90-minute, computer-based exam; mostly multiple choice. (collegeboard.com)
- DSST: Subject-area exams, formerly known as DANTES. Many colleges grant 3-6 credits per exam. Mostly multiple choice. (getcollegecredit.com)

Equivalence Exams

One other exam, the General Equivalency Diploma (GED), was designed as a substitute for a high school diploma. There is no legal requirement to take the GED in addition to completing high school, as the federal government in a 1998 amendment to the Higher Education Act (HEA) stated that homeschool parents may certify that their student has completed school for the purposes of admission to the military or obtaining financial aid. However, a few colleges and the NCAA like to see a GED even for students who have a transcript showing completed high school requirements, but many will accept other standardized-test scores instead.

- GED: This exam is administered to students over age 16. It tests for approximately 10th grade skills in Reasoning Through Language Arts, Mathematical Reasoning, Science, and Social Studies. Not recommended unless required. (ged.com)

Seven Strategies for a Successful First Year at College

Professor Carol Reynolds

They are off to college. Or they soon will be. Whether the student attends the local community college, or travels across the country to a traditional four-year school, a long-pursued goal is within reach. Now it's time to help your daughter or son to envision actually being in college. Teens may find it hard to imagine or foresee the new experiences and, yes, the problems that will need solving. So let me offer seven suggestions to help ward off some of the challenges that child will face in that all-critical freshman year.

You can think of these suggestions as strategies, as points of advice, or as warnings. But this I can promise: considering and observing them, one by one, will help ensure a student's success. Also, depending on your own educational background, some of the points may surprise you, while others will seem self-evident. But remember, we are talking about 17- and 18-year olds who are not yet fully adult. The "obvious" to a parent often hits the blind spot in a teen's understanding. Finally, you may doubt that certain things I describe here (or in my recent book *Why Freshmen Fail and How to Avoid It*) actually happen on today's college campus. But let me assure you, everything I write arises from mentoring my own students across decades of university teaching, as well as from situations I encountered in college, albeit many years ago. So let's get started.

1. The Ideal versus Reality

Recognize that your (and your child's) ideals about going to college may be vastly different from the reality of being there. Parents' ideals include seeing the child flourishing in well taught, interesting classes where the focus is on student learning. They see their children ensconced in a library, inspired by the tutelage of wise professors. They presume that the lovely landscaping and glittering buildings featured in the brochures reflect a compassionate administration and properly run academic departments. But the reality of today's college can be far removed from these ideals.

Did you ever, while encouraging your child's path to college, discuss what it might feel like to be shut out of desired courses (particularly if they are required courses)? Or have a professor who is hostile towards the subject or even the students themselves? Has your child imagined being one of two hundred students in a lecture hall where the professor appears only sporadically, whilst the class sessions are conducted by teaching assistants, some of whom, despite their kindness and academic brilliance, hail from places across the globe and struggle to speak clear English. How will your children respond if they have to stay up all night to complete assignments that were not posted in a timely manner? Have they envisioned confronting exams that contain material never assigned? For that matter, have they considered what to do if their papers are not returned . . . or even graded?

If this sounds sloppy and unprofessional, it is. Should your child be so fortunate as to avoid these problems, then count your blessings. But to a shocking degree, such things happen on today's campus. And they happen with impunity, I might add. A parent needs to discuss these possibilities with the college-bound student. And if the parent has never encountered (or cannot imagine) such situations, then find others who have. (Or consult *Why Freshmen Fail* or write directly to me, and I will be happy to share examples!) Mostly, you will want to help you child realize that "ideals" are just that: ideals. Many things we experience in our lives have to be reassessed once they stop being an ideal and become a reality.

2. Arrive Rested

Students need to arrive to the first semester of college well-rested. Optimally, they need a chance to reflect during the summer months before they launch into the demanding pace that will characterize their college years. This may sound simple to do, but it is not. High school graduates, particularly those coming out of prestigious brick-and-mortar schools, have usually spent four years on an exhausting treadmill of AP courses, demanding extra-curricular obligations interlaced with church activities and weekend jobs. Homeschooled students often enjoy the benefit of a more reasonable schedule, with better sleep and more regular meals, but they too are subject to the same scheduling fatigue. And while that summer between high school and college sounds leisurely, it can become a marathon of visiting family, engaging in one last mission trip or sports camp, or taking on-line college classes to "get ahead." High school graduates also feel the pressure to work extra hours, earning as much money as possible. The push is on.

After all that, there is the whirlwind of packing up, saying good bye, and arriving excitedly to school for the elaborate, sometimes exhausting activities of Freshmen Orientation week, which can add to the fatigue. After all of that, regular classes begin. But wait. What happened? This new daily rhythm of life is just that: a daily rhythm. And not even all that new! A freshman might think. "After all of this fuss, am I merely supposed to go to class, go back to the dorm, and study? Where did all of the excitement go?" A let down is not uncommon. In fact, you would be surprised how often this phenomenon can affect a first-term freshman.

So, in the summer before college, consider eliminating as much unnecessary activity as you can. Try to build in some empty time on the schedule. If there is to be a family trip, plan it for a place where your teen can hike, walk the beach, or simply read and reflect on a front porch. Aim for your child arriving at college well rested, even bored (if possible). That way, the daily routine of college classes, professors, and study groups will deliver the long-promised excitement.

3. Prepare to Deal with "Unfair"

Young people today hear the word "fair" an enormous amount. So much effort is put into insuring that the circumstances they face are "fair." This is especially true in homes where parents are home educators. They frequently go out of their way to treat different siblings equally, particularly making sure assignments and tests are fair. Well (ahem), in the real world, things are not fair. Parents, it is critical that you spend time with your college-bound child, explaining just how unfair the world is. As adults, we learn to take these experiences of unfairness in stride. But as teenagers coming out of a loving home where people are responsible and responsive, or as high school graduates used to benefiting from well-organized and properly administered curricula, your children will be shocked by the unfair situations that may await them in college.

Parents, start by sharing the situations you have lived through, particularly within the work place. For example, it is not uncommon to be asked by a manager to do the work of other employees who might be on leave, and yet never be compensated (or even properly thanked)? Think of all the times (not just on the job, but also in community or church work) that a so-called group project gets left to just one or two persons to complete. And yet each member of the group gets the credit. Or, think how often a boss can move up a deadline or drastically change the expectations without warning and then be angry when it is impossible to accomplish the work. None of this is fair. And things will not be fair in college. Your child may be enrolled in a section of Freshman Rhetoric that requires a serious paper every week, while her roommate's professor assigns only occasional, casual essays. Yet both girls will be awarded the same credit, despite the unfair amount of effort required to earn the grade.

For this type of situation it may be useful to consider one the best examples of an "unfair" workload ever written: the Parable of the Workers in the New Testament (Matthew, Chapter 20). The laborers who were hired at the very end of the day are awarded the same wages as those who toiled for the entire day. How fair is this? Still, even if your child is "okay" with the concept of unfair situations, these bumps in the road can affect a student's outlook. On a different note, what happens if a test on Chapters 11 and 12 also includes material from Chapter 13? Is that fair? No. Can the student protest? Yes, but not every professor will say "Oh, goodness, that is my mistake. Thank you for pointing that out. I will not count those questions against any of you."

Actually that would have been my response, had such a situation happened. But help your student realize that a professor can dismiss your child's concern, be angry about being asked, or come up with a watery explanation like "I always expect my students to read ahead." In short, I sometimes, semi-jokingly, recommend that parents prepare their children by launching a series of "Random Acts of Unfairness." Of course, I do not really advocate that you be unfair or unkind to your children. But it might be good to spring a few unfair situations on your high schoolers so that they gain experience with encountering them. At the very least, you might (depending on your children) try to initiate some "unfair" domestic situations, such as turning to your son and saying, "You did such a great job with laundry last week. I know it's supposed to be your sister's turn, but why do not you do it again this week. After all, you did such a great job." Then, turn a deaf ear on his complaints. If you try this tactic, do it as kindly as possible, and with a philosophical shrug of your shoulders, saying, "I know, I know, so many things in life are unfair, but we all are at our best when we pull together" etc., etc. At the very least, your child is more likely to smile knowingly when this kind of situation arises in real life.

4. Beware the Deceptive Freedom of a College Schedule

Repeat after me: There are no days between Thursday and Tuesday. What does this mean? Of course there are days. But in the realm of organizing one's study and personal schedule in college, the blocks of time that look blissfully "free" are, in fact, not free! Formulas vary, but a good college syllabus presumes generous hours of study time required for each hour of class time. This time might be spent translating texts, studying vocabulary, learning structural principles, researching scholarly theories, drafting and writing papers, or (most difficult) covering long lists of assigned bibliography. But the time needs to be spent.

No one (no tutor, no mom, no fellow-student) will be telling the new freshman when or how to accomplish all of this implied work. And some of the work required for a college course does look invisible or vague to a first-year student. "Did he really mean 'Read all those articles on the bibliography'?" "Are we supposed to learn every one of these terms?" "She never talks about the chapters on the syllabus, so are we really supposed to read them?" The student who draws the wrong conclusion to these questions (i.e. "no") will pay a price before the term ends. So plant the idea that, almost always, the professor expects what the syllabus says.

Those blocks of "free time" in the schedule are already filled with study, research, projects, labs, papers, and whatever else is required. And what's required is reviewing and planning the assignments due for the next class immediately at the conclusion of each class (if at all possible). It means beginning the work for next Tuesday's class on Thursday afternoon. And it means never viewing long periods of free time as anything other than a schedule for studying, with certain breaks worked in for shopping, laundry, and an occasional personal outing. I know. It sounds harsh, but at least for the Freshman year, anything else is a sure formula for academic disaster.

5. A Deadline is a Deadline

This piece of advice concerns a single issue. It's particularly relevant for students who have been homeschooled, so listen up. Think how many times throughout high school your deadlines have been changed. In fact, the flexibility to change deadlines or curricular plans is one of the great advantages of home education. A desire to explore new directions and incorporate new material, an unexpected great opportunity or crisis that throws the schedule off— these can be accommodated in the most advantageous way due to the fact that homeschooling allows flexibility. But virtually all deadlines in college will be fixed. Ordinarily, the student will be receiving an inflexible schedule with test days and paper due dates specified (unless, as unfortunately can happen, the professor tarries in posting this critical information). The only one able to change deadlines will be the professor. And if changes are made, the student will not necessarily like them.

Professors are known to move things up (to accommodate their own professional or academic schedule) or to reschedule due dates or exams for the same reason. Either one of these actions can cause a student stress. Professors are also known to add extra material to exams or increase assignments with very little warning. A delayed deadline may initially sound positive to a freshman.

"Great! More time to study" (or not to study). But delaying deadlines can cause new problems that are not immediately apparent. For example, the student may find (even without a postponed deadline) that two papers are due on the same date, with an exam scheduled early the following morning. If deadlines are delayed (particularly towards the end of a semester), scheduling overlaps are likely to get worse. So take a hard look at how the student's schedule has been handled in the past. Then have a serious discussion, and try to prepare your child for a world in which deadlines mean deadlines, and where the flexibility that may have been enjoyed in the past will be gone.

6. What is a Professor Anyway?

When I give talks about this topic, I open by saying something that might sound a bit silly: "Your professor is not Aunt Betty, nor is she your Sunday School teacher. She may be someone's mom, but she is not your mom." Audiences titter, but this is actually a serious statement. Students, particularly homeschooled students, are used to teachers who approach them like treasures who will be a delight to mentor. You child may be exactly that, but I can tell you this, for sure: few, if any, professors will look at a first-year student that way. In fact, schools factor in an attrition rate. They assume that a percentage of the freshman class will leave or flunk out. And the sooner that group is identified and moves on, the better.

Beyond that, be prepared for some professorial behavior to be unnerving, shocking, or disappointing. Professors are subject to a variety of stresses that will be new to most high schoolers, and definitely new to homeschoolers. Clearly this is a big topic, but I will give you the main points. A professor's life will have been shaped by a system called "tenure." Tenure means that a newly hired professors have only a short period of time to prove their indispensable value to the university or be fired.

In this system, good teaching is not rewarded. Publications and the ability to get grants fuel the "tenure" machine. Plus, even a professor who produces high-profile research has no guarantee that tenure will be granted. Increasingly, it is not. Add to that the fact that most professors earn modest salaries (particularly in the Liberal Arts). Workloads (number of courses taught, students assigned) are not equally distributed. Departmental politics can be extraordinarily vicious. Professors also have limited job mobility. Once granted tenure, professors frequently end up staying in one school for their whole career. There are advantages to this, but also disadvantages, starting with professional stagnation. All of these issues can affect your teen's experience, but most teenagers will likely never have thought of these issues, or will not be equipped to understand them without help.

7. Remember to Show Up, a.k.a. Prepare for the Temptation to Skip Classes

This is one of those points that seem obvious (as mentioned at the beginning of this article). Of course I will be going to class, says your child, with utmost sincerity. If only it were that simple! Very few 18-year olds can imagine the double-whammy of experiencing the loss of parental control over their day-to-day actions while staring at a menu of attractive, often dazzling opportunities (or temptations), vying for their time and energy. Furthermore, depending on the school or even the academic department, the freshman may encounter a culture that says: "Going to class is boring/ unimportant/ unnecessary/superfluous." Your child is likely to hear apparently success-ful upperclassmen gently ridicule the practice of going to every class: "That professor never does anything except read her PowerPoint and she posts it all on line." Or, "All the questions from the test come from his handouts. Why bother to drag yourself out of bed on a cold, rainy November morning to go to class?"

Why indeed? Classes in some disciplines can indeed be boring, and students may feel they are learning nothing that is not printed in a textbook or posted in on-line study guides. But going to class is never a waste of time. Even if a student merely watches the clock, or counts the number of bricks in the wall, being present at class time is important for at least four reasons:

- They will not be violating a written, or unwritten, attendance policy for the class. (Yes, professors and Teaching Assistants do notice and can record absences, even if rolls are not called and no attendance policy is stated in the syllabus.)
- Surprise announcements, such as changing due dates or revising the chapters covered for a test, will likely be made primarily or solely in class. And you cannot count on fellow students to tell you these things, even if you think you can.
- You will figure out (if you try) the degree of seriousness with which the professor regards the course (a blow-off lark or unpleasant interruption to the professor's other-wise dynamic life versus an expression of long-held personal interest and dedication). You can assess these critical things only if you are there.
- You will get at least some information as to what questions are likely to be asked on an exam. Class attendance allows the student to glean the professor's preferred ap-proaches to many things, including studying for exams, constructing term papers, or assembling class presentations.

There is a fifth reason, too. Whether you are paying for your education yourself or a scholarship fund is, someone is paying the per/class tuition for you to be there. Take the costs of the course, divide it by how many credit hours it yields, and divide that amount by the number of class sessions. The resulting amount is what each class session is costing you (or someone—a scholarship foundation or loan organization). The answer is simple. Never, ever miss a class unless the reason is overwhelmingly strong (e.g., a 103-degree fever, a death in the family, a canceled flight). Just don't do it.

§

Well, now you have my seven suggestions. Consider them, talk them over with your child, and share them other family members or friends who have a college background. See what kind of a response you get. Along those lines, encourage your child to solicit as many stories about "mistakes" in college as people are willing to share, because, despite how it seems, children do take in what they are told. And remember, Mom and Dad's voices may not be at hand every day to guide and guard, as they so long were. But the years of nurturing and training, plus the collective wisdom of those who have trodden this path before them, can resonate in students' ears. And every time it does, there is a good chance an avoidable mistake will be avoided. And, quicker than you think, that critical freshman year will be traversed and conquered!

About Professor Carol

Professor Carol Reynolds spent over 20 years as a Music History professor at Southern Methodist University in Dallas, TX. Since retiring, she has been teaching homeschoolers, concert audiences, and travelers about the fine arts. For decades, she has served as an educator for arts organizations, including the Dallas Symphony and the Van Cliburn Foundation. Fluent in Russian and German, Dr. Reynolds has led educational tours to Russia, Germany, and arts centers in the US. Now on behalf of the Smithsonian Institute she speaks to audiences in the Holy Land, the Caribbean, and across the Atlantic, and leads arts tours to Eastern Europe.

In addition to *Why Freshman Fail*, Dr. Reynolds is the author of the homeschool multi-media courses *Discovering Music: 300 Years of Interaction in Western Music, Arts, History, and Culture; Exploring America's Musical Heritage;* and *Early Sacred Music*, which covers Early Christian liturgical music from the Temple in Jerusalem through the Middle Ages. You will find her courses and other resources at ProfessorCarol. com.

College Alternatives

Not every student is called to a profession that requires college. Not every student is ready for college right out of high school. Not every student is able to benefit from a four year college degree. College can be a wonderful learning experience for an engaged, motivated student, but for some, it's just an expensive party venue with a long-lasting bill.

If you have students who maintain they do not need college, do not want it, or do not understand the purpose and meaning of education, it is probably not the right time for that student to go to college. It is better to wait until they are ready than to rush off right after high school and incur debt for an education they will not appreciate. They can go to work, start a business, work on the family farm, or do something else. If they eventually need college, it will be there.

Skilled trades

One of the best college alternatives is a skilled trade. The trades include skilled labor jobs such as machinist, mechanic, builder, welder, electrician, pipe fitter, plumber, glazier, stone mason, cabinet maker, and machine maintenance personnel as well as non-industrial jobs such as baker, medical assistant, dental hygienist, mortician, arborist, midwife, legal secretary, and many others. My husband and I encouraged our sons to cultivate both a white-collar head skill and a blue-collar hand skill, not just to have backup career options, but for wholeness of spirit. Although each has a bent toward one type of skill or another, having experience in both has been a personal and professional plus for each of them.

College is a great place to expand the knowledge and thinking skills that make life richer, but the trades offer a clear path to the workforce. The trades experience chronic labor shortages, which are only getting worse as experienced workers retire. According to an article in Fortune, "companies that make tangible products are struggling to find candidates for about 237,000 job openings. To put that figure in perspective, it's 89,000 more than the entire U.S. economy created in September." Those openings need to be filled, and a 2013 article in Forbes analyzes where the greatest needs will be in the coming years. If you are willing to consider a career based on demand, the article offers solid, though slightly dated, statistics to consider. Many people who work in the trades by day continue to study and read for personal development in other parts of their life, so opting for a trade does not mean that education ends at high school.

Wages for the skilled trades have been compared to wages for middle managers, but figures vary, depending on experience and where you live. Forbes suggest that the "median wage . . . is $20.25 an hour, and even the bottom 10 percent earn $13.14 an hour." Best of all, the work done in most trades can be confined to the paid work day, meaning that under normal circumstances an employed trades-person is not expected to be accessible by phone or email during off hours or vacations (it is different for business owners or first responders, of course). Being able to leave work at work reduces stress and makes it possible to spend time in things that matter—family, service in the community, and so forth. Training for the skilled trades can come through vocational training programs, trade schools, community colleges, or apprenticeships. The lower costs of training, coupled with the labor shortage in many of the trades, makes them an excellent college alternative or secondary career.

Interestingly, Matthew Crawford in *Shop Class as Soulcraft* writes of anecdotal evidence that suggests "one of the fastest-growing segments of the student body at community colleges is people who already have a four-year degree and return to get a marketable trade skill" (p. 12). Subtitled "An Inquiry into the Value of Work," *Shop Class as Soulcraft* examines the purpose, meaning, and value of productive labor through the lens of Crawford's transition from think-tank PhD to motorcycle mechanic. He makes a compelling case for the trades, noting that he has "often found manual work more engaging intellectually" than wrestling with the abstract. As an additional plus, there is even an extra bit of job security for some of the trades—when was the last time you heard of a plumbing job being outsourced to China?

Relevant Articles Online

- www.forbes.com/sites/emsi/2013/03/07/americas-skilled-trades-dilemma-shortages-loom-as-most-in-demand-group-of-workers-ages/#266bf2c46397
- www.pbs.org/newshour/education/decades-pushing-bachelors-degrees-u-s-needs-tradespeople

Resources for information on the trades

- *Profoundly Disconnected* is Mike Rowe's site, designed to "challenge the absurd belief that a four-year degree is the only path to success." Good articles and information, well presented. (profoundlydisconnected.com)

- MikeRoweWORKSFoundationScholarshipOpportunities:Herearelinkstopartnerships andscholarshipopportunitiesforhighschoolseniorswantingtolearnaskill. (profound-lydisconnected.com/the-mikeroweworks-foundation-scholarship-opportunities)

- You can find detailed information about all sorts of jobs in the *Occupational Outlook Handbook*, a free database from the Bureau of Labor Statistics. (bls.gov/ooh)

- The U.S. Department of Labor offers good information on job training. (www.dol. gov/general/topic/training)

- Check your state's Department of Labor for information about jobs and apprenticeship programs. For example, search online for your state name and DOL, e.g. "Virginia DOL."

- The federal government gives grants to community and faith-based programs to provide job training. You can read the press releases on the site to find programs in your area. (www.dol.gov/cfbnp)

- National Center for Construction Education and Research offers information and certification. (www.nccer.org)

- Some labor unions offer excellent paid training programs; just search for them by trade and state. I recommend reading all the fine print of any agreement, as well as the organization's constitution, before getting involved. Use this international list of unions to locate programs of interest. (en.wikipedia.org/wiki/List_of_trade_unions)

- To learn more about workforce training programs in your state, do an online search for "workforce initiative [state name]".

- If you would like to read more about labor shortages in the trades, do an online search for "labor shortages trades." Some articles contain useful links and resources.

Entrepreneurship, Apprenticeships, and Guilds

The trades may not be for everyone, but entrepreneurship, apprenticeships, or guilds provide other alternatives. Even if your student eventually decides to attend college, he or she can benefit by having one or more of these experiences during high school.

Entrepreneurship: Microbusiness

One way students can experiment with entrepreneurship is to start a microbusiness while still in high school. A microbusiness (or micro-business) is a very small business that offers a product or service. It is started with minimal resources, and operates without business loans or major overhead. Microbusnesses are ideal for teens who want to save for college while gaining business skills. They also work well for work-at-home moms or people who need to make money while caregiving for elderly family members. A microbusiness can also be a good way to try out a possible career, or to supplement income.

Microbusiness possibilities are nearly endless. My own microbusiness career began when I was in elementary school—I used my little red wagon to peddle avocados around our neighborhood. I made an average of $100 a season until I felt too grown-up to be seen in public with a red wagon. I graduated to making macramé bracelets with beaded names; then to doing—and ultimately teaching—calligraphy. Each of these microbusinesses brought in a decent amount of money for doing something fun and relatively low-key. I am certain that the skills I learned from each venture were more valuable than almost anything I would have gained in a traditional minimum-wage job.

If you would like to explore microbusiness with your teens, you will find the four-book *Micro Business for Teens* curriculum by Carol Topp to be a clear, concise guide (MicrobusinessCurriculum.com). Carol is not only a homeschool mom; she is also a Certified Public Accountant (CPA) who has worked with many adult and teen entrepreneurs. If your teen works through the curriculum and successfully launches and runs a business, you can add credit for Entrepreneurship 101 to their high school transcript. Each book builds upon the previous one, developing the business skills necessary for success. The four titles are:

- *Starting a Microbusiness*
- *Running a Microbusiness*
- *Money and Taxes in a Microbusiness*
- *Microbusiness for Teens Workbook*

Apprenticeships and Guilds

Although I would like to report that formal apprenticeships are easy to find, a recent Wall Street Journal article, "Apprenticeships Help Close the Skills Gap. So Why Are They in Decline?"

suggests otherwise. Although classic apprenticeship programs allow employers to train for precisely the needed skill set for a position, they have traditionally been seen as more of a blue-collar option. In addition, some employers fear that an apprenticeship program may open the way for unionization (labor unions provide some of the best apprenticeship programs available).

However, an apprenticeship can be well worth pursuing. According to Brad Neese, director of Apprenticeship Carolina, a program of the South Carolina Technical College System, employers who provide apprenticeship programs discover that "College degrees and internships do not produce the same quality of worker as intensive, on-the-job apprenticeships." Many homeschoolers have found informal apprenticeships through acquaintances and local contacts, as described in some of the articles below. One of the easiest ways to begin is to offer services on a volunteer basis. Sometimes this will work into a paying position; other times it simply provides experience.

- The Vocational Information Center has excellent links and resources: (ww.khake. com/page58.html)

- The Apprenticeship site from the U.S. Department of Labor provides a place where employers can offer apprenticeships, students can search for opportunities, and parents and potential partners can learn more. (www.dol.gov/apprenticeship)

- Medieval Guilds from Thomas More College "Inspired by the original models, Thomas More College has established a series of guilds that enable students to gain practical skills and experience in areas such as woodworking, sacred art, homesteading and music." (www.thomasmorecollege.edu/student-life/catholic-guilds/)

- What Do Homeschoolers Do After Graduation? Here is a dated but interesting look at what some Pennsylvania homeschoolers have done after college, along with some practical advice and comments from parents on things that worked well in their homeschooling. (www.pahomeschoolers.com/newsletter/issue66.htm)

- The National Institute for Metalworking Skills, Inc. (NIMS} Competency Based Apprenticeship System offers the opportunity to become a NIMS Certified Machinist, Toolmaker, CNC Setup Programmer or a Certified Journey Worker at any NIMS occupation. (nims-skills.org/apprenticeship)

- Arborist Training Programs links to some useful resources for tree climbers. You may find more by searching online for "arborist apprenticeship programs." (natlarb.com/ arborist-training-information)

- AFL-CIO apprenticeship information: In general, unions offer extensive, well-paid apprenticeship options in a number of fields. (aflcio.org/about-us/ careers-and-apprenticeships)

A Sampling of Small or Local Opportunities

- Many small, local companies and organizations offer apprenticeship or internship opportunities. These can be well worth pursuing, as they can open doors to local career opportunities. Try searching online for opportunities in your area by entering "apprenticeship [city name]" or "internship [city name]." You may also add in the field in which you would like to find on-the-job training—technology, farm work, plumbing, etc.. If your student can shadow a well-respected adult and learn by doing, it is likely to be an experience he will not forget.

- Homegrown Programmers is an apprenticeship program offered by the homeschooling owners of Automation Excellence, a technology company. (homegrownprogrammers.com/apprenticeships)

- Agriberry Farm offers a Young Worker Training Program in central Virginia. (agriberry.com/hiring/ywtp-summer-seasonal)

- Joel Salatin's Polyface Farm has a popular apprenticeship program for "Bright eyed, bushy-tailed, self-starter, eager-beaver, situationally aware, go-get-'em, teachable, positive, non-complaining, grateful, rejoicing, get'erdone, dependable, faithful, perseverant take-responsibility, clean-cut, all American boy-girl appearance characters. We are very, very, very discriminatory." Working with the bright and opinionated Salatin is bound to be a life-changing experience for any teen interested in permaculture. (polyfacefarms.com/apprenticeship)

- Quivira Coalition lists agrarian ranch apprenticeships in the western United States. (quiviracoalition.org/apprenticeships)

- Greenville Technical College is partnering with GE Power & Water to develop skilled machinists through the GE Gas Turbine Machinist Apprentice Program. (gvltec.edu/GE-apprentice)

You will find that some states have more opportunities than others. To locate more of these, search online with terms such as those below, adding your state name:

- machinist apprenticeship programs
- ranch apprenticeship programs
- technical apprenticeship programs
- automotive apprenticeship programs
- arborist apprenticeship programs

You get the idea—if your teen is interested in creative, on-the-job learning, just start asking around locally or search online. There are options available you never dreamed of!

Military

Joining the military can provide a way to serve the country while obtaining education, certifications, and more, mostly through on the job training. Each branch of service—Army, Navy, Air Force, Marines, Coast Guard, National Guard, and the Reserves division of each of these—offers a different focus, atmosphere, and benefits. Depending on whether a student is interested in Officer Training School or just enlisting, there are very different prerequisites and requirements for entry. Because information changes regularly, I will just point you to two excellent, authoritative sources that will always be current.

- A good place to begin research is the Today's Military website. Here you can find user-friendly information about each branch of service and its requirements. (todaysmilitary.com)
- The U.S. government provides basic information and links to each service. (www.usa.gov/join-military)

Six Things Your Teen Can Do While Homeschooling High School

Get a Jump Start on College

Why spend four years just doing high school, when you could exert a little extra effort and earn college credit at the same time? By taking advantage of college-level exams, community college and online classes, and other opportunities, it's possible to graduate from college when most teens are graduating from high school.

Serve Others Through Volunteering

I have heard it said that teenagers are old enough to be useful, but young enough to be dangerous. One thing that can help a teen through this awkward stage of life is serving others. There are countless volunteer opportunities, formal and informal, within the church and community. Homeschooled teens have the opportunity to learn while meeting real needs for real people.

Start a Microbusiness

What could be better than a summer job flipping burgers? Entrepreneurship, for one thing. Just think—instead of spending time in a mindless entry-level job, teens can start and run a small business, and not only earn money for the future, but also learn about planning, budgeting, organization, marketing, and customer service, and perhaps even gain experience for a future career.

Do Career Sampling or an Apprenticeship

In traditional school, you are lucky to get one day off each year to shadow a worker at his or her job. Homeschooled teens can try different careers through informal mentoring relationships, formal apprenticeships, or volunteering opportunities.

Develop Special Talents

Have you noticed who has been winning spelling and geography bees, music competitions and chess tournaments, debates and robotics competitions? Homeschooled students are often at the very top of these contests. Why? It's because they have time to pursue special interests. If they want to spend three hours a day practicing violin, there are few deadlines. They do not have to put down their instrument after 45 minutes and go rushing off to algebra or soccer.

Learn Through Travel

Just over a century ago, well-educated students were expected to complete their schooling with a Grand Tour of the world. While you may not have the resources for a Grand Tour, you can probably travel to nearby historic sites, visit other states, or, yes, even travel around the world. By preparing wisely and choosing to travel when rates are low, you can experience different cultures and make unique memories without breaking your budget. Travel can be an education all by itself!

High School Q&A

How early do I need to start planning?

Ideally, the junior-high school years can be used to map out a plan for high school, but you can start wherever you are. Just pull together information about what you have done so far, start filling out the worksheets, and go on from there.

What about "gaps"?

If you are starting to fill out the transcript when your student has almost completed school, you may notice that there are classes missing in one or more of the important academic areas. You have several options, depending upon the teen's future plans. For a college bound student, you may need to delay graduation to complete the extra classes at home, or you may decide to have the student take the needed subjects at the community college and count them as dual credit.

Does the student need an accredited diploma?

Not usually. A diploma simply acknowledges that the student has finished high school in accordance with the laws of your state, and under a 1998 amendment to the Higher Education Act (HEA), homeschooling parents may certify this in most states.

How can I teach subjects I do not remember?

Almost everyone worries about teaching something (if you want to see me turn pale, just break out an algebra textbook!), but fortunately, homeschooling through high school does not mean that you have to teach all the subjects yourself. There are many ways to learn a challenging subject—you and your student have options. Independently or together, you could:

- Learn from video courses such as the ones from GreatCourses.com (this may work best for subjects the student enjoys).
- Take an online class from outstanding teachers (e.g. Schola Classical Tutorials, Memoria Online Academy, Schole Academy, etc.).

- Follow a self-directed course or study guide such as the free curriculum guides from AmblesideOnline.org.

- Take an online course from a university. Coursera offers an extensive directory of inexpensive courses (less than $100) from top universities including Yale, Stanford, Duke, UVA, and many more. coursera.org

- Take a community college class. This can be a good way to take higher math and lab sciences—colleges usually have great lab equipment and the instructors can answer complex questions. I do not recommend taking literature there, as students are unlikely to be assigned the foundational classic works they need for cultural literacy.

- Join a local homeschool co-op that offers classes in high school subjects (your state homeschool association may maintain a list of co-ops).

- Find a tutor through a local college or tutoring service.

- Enroll in a distance learning high school such as Sycamore Academy, Oak Meadow, or Seton Home Study.

- Learn to write well with the *Student Writing Intensive* from the Institute for Excellence in Writing or the *Lost Tools of Writing* from Circe Institute.

No matter what subject your student needs to learn, there are resources and options that will help you teach it.

My homeschooler did high school algebra in seventh grade. Can I count it on the transcript?

Unless a college specifies otherwise in the instructions to applicants, you may usually record all high school work on the transcript. Colleges tend to be interested in what has been studied, not when it was studied. Always check the homeschool admission page of each individual college to be certain, though, as some want to see only what the student did during the traditional four years of school. In this case, just list the four most advanced classes in each subject area on the transcript. Some colleges will want to see the exact year when each class was taken, others do not. Again, check each college's website for college-specific advice, and do not hesitate to call the admissions office if you or your student have further questions.

Does my student have to take a foreign language?

I recommend that students take at least one year of a foreign language, even if they are not college bound. It is helpful not only in understanding the structure of English but also in the work world, where bilingual workers are increasingly needed.

Transcripts Made Easy

What about too many credits?

Some homeschoolers are faced with the problem of too many credits to fit on the traditional one-page transcript. If the college of your choice has no preference, you can choose either to weed out lower-level courses in a subject or to go with the "more is better" philosophy. In cases where the selection of extra courses indicates a special interest or talent, especially if the student has studied much more deeply or broadly than average or plans to major in the subject, it can be helpful to show all the classes. Like a magnet school's targeted curriculum, your homeschool can offer an experience tailored to the student and his or her future plans.

My student athlete wants to be eligible for the NCAA. Is this possible with homeschooling?

Yes, it is possible, and a fair number of students have accomplished it. The requirements are similar to those outlined in this book, but there are small differences. For the most current information, it is always best to check www.ncaa.org/student-athletes/future/home-school-students.

Teaching Teens

Wise thoughts from Charlotte Mason

What Must Be Taught

"First and chiefest is the **knowledge of God**, to be got at most directly through the Bible; then comes the **knowledge of man**, to be got through history, literature, art, civics, ethics, biography, the drama, and languages; and lastly, so much **knowledge of the universe** as shall explain to some extent the phenomena we are familiar with and give a naming acquaintance at any rate with birds and flowers, stars and stones; nor can this knowledge of the universe be carried far in any direction without the ordering of mathematics…"

How to Teach It

"… Believe in mind, and let education go straight as a bolt to the mind of the pupil. The use of books is a necessary corollary, because no one is arrogant enough to believe he can teach every subject … with the original thought and exact knowledge shown by the man who has written a book on … his life-study … Treat children in this reasonable way … the minds of a score of thinkers who meet the children, mind to mind, in their several books, the teacher performing the graceful office of presenting the one enthusiastic mind to the other … [There must be] a great deal of consecutive reading from very various books, all of some literary value…"

What is the Result of this Teaching?

"… The introduction of the methods I advocate has a curious effect on a whole family … The whole household thinks of and figures to itself great things, for nothing is so catching as knowledge … Children so taught are delightful companions because they have large interests and worthy thoughts; they have much to talk about and such casual talk benefits society. The fine sense, like an atmosphere, of things worth knowing and worth living for, this it is which produces magnanimous citizens, and we feel that Milton was right in claiming magnanimity as the proper outcome of education."

From "A Liberal Education in Secondary Schools" in *A Philosophy of Education* by Charlotte Mason

Charlotte Mason was a 19th-century educator whose unique philosophy and methods are extraordinarily well suited to the needs of home educators. A Charlotte Mason education is broad and deep, and centered in the use of excellent books. You can learn more and get free curriculum plans from AmblesideOnline.org.

Part 3

Keep Simple Records

The key to keeping paperwork simple is to settle on a single system and use it effectively. I tried many systems while we were homeschooling, but kept coming back to the basics, which I will outline in this chapter. These basics include the reproducible Subject Worksheets and Class Profile sheets you will find in the back of this book, plus a binder and pocket folder for each student. In addition, I suggest compiling each student's final four-year course record in a small, inexpensive record booklet such as the *High School Student Record* from the Peaceful Planning system (peacefulplanning.net), or other compact record book.

High School Binder

Begin with a large binder for each student. This becomes an easy-to-reference cumulative file, and will contain representative work samples, planning pages, and reading logs. The Student Record booklet, if you are using one, can be stored in the inside cover pocket. Use tabs to divide the binder into one section per grade.

At the beginning of each year, place a Class Profile worksheet (from the Reproducibles section at the end of this book) and a photocopy of the table of contents or pacing chart from each of the principle books or study guides that will be used for that class behind the appropriate grade tab. At the end of the year, add student work samples behind each Class Profile. Extra tabs at the back of the binder can be used for things like reading logs, standardized test results, or copies of any official documentation you are required to file for your student.

Student Work Samples to Keep

Purpose: Evidence of progress

To make grading easier and provide documentation to support the student's grades, keep a few work samples. You do not need to save boxes of student work—just representative samples from the beginning, middle, and end of the school year. The goal is to show how much your student has progressed in each subject.

We tried many ways to keep work samples during the school year, and finally settled on simple manila pocket folders. A 2" pocket folder is usually adequate for a year's worth of work samples for one student, but if you tend to keep more, they are available in sizes up to 3.5" deep. Just choose the size you prefer. If you prefer to keep the record digitally, just scan the chosen samples and save to organized folders in Google Drive or Dropbox.

Each month, add 1-2 work samples from each subject into the student's pocket folder. At the end of the semester or year, sort and review the samples. Select three good samples from each subject—one each from the beginning, middle, and end of the semester or year. Each sample should be an example of the student's best work at that time, and the three samples together should show a deepening of knowledge and skills. You will have 12-18 samples from each year, which should provide an excellent overview of educational progress.

Once you have selected the samples to keep, place them in the student's high school binder behind the tab for the correct grade. Add copies of Reading and Activity Logs if the student has been keeping these. Add brief progress notes, the date the course was completed, and a grade to the appropriate page in the Student Record booklet or whatever record keeping tool you have chosen.

Additional Planning and Record-Keeping Resources

The pocket folder, binder, reproducible forms, and record booklet form a complete long-term record-keeping system. For day-to-day plans and records, a datebook or planner can bridge the gap between personal and school planning. I use a 5½" x 8½" Traveler's Notebook style planner with Moleskine notebooks and my own custom inserts, but almost any type of organizer that offers space for weekly scheduling and notes will work. Spaces are small, so notations have to be brief and to the point, but there is space for enough information to keep a daily schedule moving. I keep a one-year overview calendar, three months' worth of weekly pages, and three notebooks, each for a different purpose, in my datebook binder. The datebook is what I take with me when I go out, while the high school binder and other records stay at home.

Reading Log

Since reading is arguably the single most important thing a student can do to educate the mind and nourish the spirit, a reading log is a very useful tool. Having the student record all reading creates an interesting record and can help you maintain a balanced reading program. A well-rounded reading list is a great supplement to a college admission essay, too. It can also be fun to look back at high school reading logs and recall favorite and not-so-favorite books. You will find a simple Reading Log form in the Reproducibles section, or your student may prefer to use a journal or a computer file. I like things compact, so I have small reading log booklets that have space to record 100 books at PeacefulPlanning.net. Whichever you choose, be sure the writing in the record is legible.

Activities Log

If your student participates in structured extracurricular activities such as sports, debate, Scouting, robotics, drama, music, etc., it is a good idea to record them, as some may count toward course credit on the transcript. As with the Reading Log, it is best if the student does the recording. The Activities Log worksheet in the Reproducibles section has space to list each activity, the date, and the amount of time involved. At the end of each semester, you will be able to add up the time spent and know when the student has accumulated enough time to earn credit for the activity.

You can also record activities such as hobbies, sports, or vocational training, as well as academic events (science fairs, debate club, and so forth), for nearly everything is worth at least some credit. Remember that public schools give credit for choir, journalism, band, independent living (formerly home economics), typing, and other classes that are not strictly academic in nature. Learning is learning, and it is all valuable.

How to Use Class Profile Sheets

Purpose: Planning and draft for final record

Class Profile sheets are designed to help you plan ahead. The information you record on them will serve as a bird's-eye view of what is to be covered during a semester or year. Once you have finished the class, transfer the information, with any changes that occurred mid-year, from the Class Profile worksheet you used for planning to a fresh sheet (or to one of the Class Profile pages in the High School Record booklet mentioned earlier). It will become part of the student's final record in the high school binder.

The profiles provide backup information for the transcript if an admissions counselor wants to know exactly what was studied in a particular class. For subjects such as math, which do not usually have readings, just list the major concepts covered, using the textbook table of contents or syllabus for reference.

Sample Class Profile: What's On It, and Why

On the next page you will see a sample Class Profile worksheet, using course information from the Excellence in Literature curriculum (English IV: British Literature—ExcellenceInLiterature. com). Notice that I included only the focus texts in the list of readings. There are many shorter items called "context readings" that are also assigned, but these are brief and too numerous for the Class Profile, which outlines only the focus and major activities from the course.

Timing and additional details for this class are outlined on the pacing chart from the study guide (remember, the pacing chart would have been photocopied and placed in the High School Binder where you are keeping the student's cumulative records). Course assignments are also described only briefly on this sheet, because more information is on the pacing chart. Remember, this profile is only a bird's-eye view—complete details are not necessary.

Class Profile (Sample)

Class: Excellence in Lit: English IV, British Literature   **Date:** Fall 2030

Description: This is the first semester of a two-semester course studying classic British Literature chronologically and in historical and cultural context. There is an honors option available with extra reading and a research assignment at the end of the year; we will decide whether to do this after the semester begins.

Outside Resources/Tutors: None.

Final Grade/Comments:

Readings	Assignments
• Module 1 - Middle English: Beowulf	Author Profile for each unit
• Module 2- Selections from Canterbury Tales by Geoffrey Chaucer	•1- Beowulf: Historical Approach paper; Retell as modern prose or write analytical essay
• Module 3 - Edmund Spenser, Sir Gawain and the Green Knight, and the Arthurian Legend	•2- Canterbury Tales: Middle English exercise; 750-word comparison essay
• Module 4 – King Lear by William Shakespeare	•3- Sir Gawain: Approach Paper; Faerie Queene: Record epigraphs; Analytical essay on 1 of 2 topics
• Module 5 – Paradise Lost by John Milton	•4- Scene summaries; Compare/contrast essay
• Module 6 – Pride and Prejudice by Jane Austen	•5- Summarize each book in the epic; Analytical essay on 1 of 2 topics
• Module 7 - Great Expectations by Charles Dickens	•6- Letter-writing exercise; Poetry analysis or analytical essay
• Module 8 – Wuthering Heights by Emily Brontë	•7- Approach paper & character essay
• Module 9- To the Lighthouse by Virginia Woolf	•8-Journalism exercise; Analytical essay on 1 of 2 topics
•Context readings from Norton Anthology, library and online resources	•9- Approach paper or retelling; Analytical essay on 1 of 2 topics
•Poets studied include Donne, Herbert, Marvell, and others	•Dynamic Literacy Word Build

Grading: Course grade will be based upon essays (70%), shorter assignments (15%), vocabulary (5%), and studentship (10%).

How to Use Subject Worksheets

Purpose: A catch-all worksheet to organize activities by subject

The Subject Worksheets are what you use to record extra, non-traditional or brief educational activities for possible inclusion in one or more of the student's credit-earning classes. You can also briefly note all classes and major standardized exams the student completes. For each course listed, be sure to add the earned units to the total of units earned at the top of the sheet

I have provided a reproducible worksheet for each of the primary areas of study in the back of the book. Each worksheet has space to briefly identify the course or event, and relevant details. When you are ready to create the transcript, many of these extra activities and hours can be added to classes you have outlined on Class Profile sheets, or even combined to make an entirely new elective. Once you have made notes on these sheets, filling out the actual transcript should be pretty easy.

So What Goes on the Subject Worksheets?

- Academic contests such as debate, robotics, or Math Olympiad
- Participation in community based arts such as theatre, Junior Philharmonic, etc.
- Unit-study projects
- Lab experiments
- Academically focused field trips
- Co-op or dual-credit classes
- AP or college-level exams
- Scouting, 4-H, and other community-based experiences
- Choir, instrumental music, missions, and other church-based activities
- Learning experiences gained through work, travel, or volunteer service

How to List Unit Studies on the Worksheets

If you use unit studies, remember that some activities may fit into more than one category, so you may end up with several fractions of a credit placed on different Subject Worksheets. For example, if your student spends a semester researching and writing about the history of Britain with a focus on the kings and queens of England, you could assign a ½ credit of English or of history, or ¼ credit each. Purchased unit studies such as *Tapestry of Grace* usually specify exactly how much credit is earned for each of the topics covered.

Sample Subject Worksheet: What's On It, and Why

On the next page is a sample of a Subject Worksheet for the subject of English. You will notice there are several entry categories on the worksheet. At the top of the worksheet, the subject is identified, and basic information such as the number of units needed and earned to meet high school requirements for that subject, is summarized. This is followed by the body of the worksheet, in which you see a variety of items recorded: a standard English class; a college-level exam; a writing contest; a co-op class, a field trip, and more. This is the type of information you will want to record for each subject. You do not need daily details or class-content information, as the individual course content will be summarized on the Class Profile sheets.

At the end of the year, review the Subject Worksheets to see if any of the courses, exams, or activities can be included in credit for one of the student's other classes. For students who have a strong interest in pursuing a hobby such as carving, hiking, musical performance, or robotics, the hours of learning and experience accumulated on a Subject Worksheet in that area may end up being enough for an elective. In that case, simply transfer all the related experiences from the Subject Worksheet to a Class Profile for the student's final records.

Subject Worksheet: English (Sample)

High school units required: State____4___ College____4___ Other _____

Units earned: Grade _____ 9 –1 Grade _____ 10 –1.5_ Grade ____11 –1.5 Grade 12 _____

College-level credits earned: Total _____ By Exam –6 _____ Class –3 _____

Hours Spent or Units Earned	Description of Class, Test, or Activity	Grade	Date	Test Score	Notes
1	Literature and Composition (Excellence in Literature English 2)	A	Sept/June 2024-25		
1 unit; 6 coll. credits	Analysis and Interpretation of Literature (CLEP)	A**	Fall 2026	79/90	Used this as a final exam for the Honors Option of EIL.
½	Comparative Literature: Allegory, Myth, & Fantasy from Ancient to Modern Times	A	Spring 2024		Co-op class taken with the Great Books Circle.
7 hours	Writer's Digest Contest: Entered short story.				Won honorable mention in online story contest; teen division.
½	Survey of the Short Story: Norton Anthology of Short Fiction	A	Fall 2025		
1 -1/2 days	Field trip to Edgar Allen Poe museum; blog post and 3-page report.		10/16/2025		Add to American Literature Class Profile as part of credit.
1 unit; 3 coll. Credits	English Literature to 1688 (JSRCC)	A**	Spr. 2026		Did not care for literature selections; supplemented with EIL British Literature.

*** Dual-credit courses or honors classes will earn weighted grade points.*

Naming Classes

Students who follow a traditional curriculum do not usually have much trouble naming classes. However, if you have put together your own curriculum, or if you are a relaxed homeschooler or an unschooler, one challenge you will face is translating unconventional learning experiences into descriptive class names. Once you get going, however, you will find that it is easy, and can even be fun.

Basic Ideas for Naming

You can keep things simple by sticking with the basics, though this does not provide much information about what the class included. You can call your classes any of the following:

- Subject plus year (English 9, 10, 11, 12)
- Subject plus a Roman numeral (History I, II, III, IV)
- Specific subject name (Biology, English Literature, Chinese History)
- Textbook or program name (Video-Text Algebra, Rosetta Stone French I)
- Publisher and subject (Memoria Press Latin I, Tapestry of Grace World History, Excellence in Literature English IV: World Literature)
- Author and subject (Jay Wile Chemistry)
- Curriculum provider and subject (Sonlight 20th Century History, John Tyler Community College Biology I)

Beyond that, you may find additional ideas at high school and college websites, as well as college catalogs. College class descriptions are usually more focused and specific than those at the high school level, so they are also a good place to look for inspiration.

Advanced Naming Ideas

The National Center for Education Statistics (NCES) publishes a useful guide on naming and describing courses. The *Secondary School Course Classification System* is designed to provide high schools across the nation with a wide array of course names and descriptions (there is one for primary grades as well). It is available as a free, downloadable PDF at nces.ed.gov/pubsearch/pubsinfo.asp?pubid=2007341 (or just do an Internet search for the title). These course names and descriptions can be used exactly as they are written or adapted to your needs. Even if you do not use many of them, they are a great source for creative class ideas.

Getting Specific With Course Names

If you want to be more specific or creative, there are many ways you can list a class or activity. For example, a teen who has built a baby sitting business may have taken Red Cross courses in childcare and first aid, learned about business record-keeping, and read up on how to incorporate simple educational activities and crafts. "Babysitting 101" would not only fail to convey the breadth of the student's learning and experience, but it would also not look very impressive on a transcript. Therefore, you may want to grant credit or fractions of a credit using more academic-sounding course names.

One possibility from the *Secondary School Course Classification System* is #19052: "Child Development." According to the provided course description, "Child Development classes provide students with knowledge about the physical, mental, emotional, and social growth and development of children from conception to pre-school age, emphasizing the application of this knowledge in child care settings. These courses typically include related topics such as the appropriate care of infants, toddlers, and young children."

Other possibilities for fractions of credit include:

- Fundamentals of Childcare
- Entrepreneurship 101
- Home Economics: Child Care
- Introduction to First Aid

You may even decide to separate the different activities performed in the business, list them on appropriate Subject Worksheets and grant fractions of a credit for more than one subject, based upon the number of hours spent.

Course Names for Short Courses and Non-Academic Subjects

When I was in high school, we were able to take 10-week mini-courses called "Special Modules." These were often project-based and included things such as calligraphy, woodworking, print shop, photography and film development, and film and book studies. Most were credited as electives. These short classes can be a great way to provide credit for some of the project-based learning your student experiences outside the classroom. For example, hours spent learning

HTML in order to create a web page can be listed on a Class Profile sheet as part of a course in Computer Technology or Web Design. Time spent writing, designing, and illustrating a family or school newsletter could be listed as Journalism, Graphic Design, Communication Skills, or simply added to the English Subject Worksheet as part of the student's English credit.

Students who help out on family farms will find that many experiences can be part of structured courses if the activities are written down and time is logged. Consider course number 18401: "Agriculture Mechanics/Equipment/Structures" from the *Secondary School Course Classification System*. For many teens, the things listed in the course description are simply part of the ordinary, everyday job of helping to maintain and improve the farm. From an educator's perspective, these are valuable skills that require learning and practice, so they are well worth credit. Here is the description:

> "Agriculture Mechanics/Equipment/Structures courses provide students with the skills and knowledge that are specifically applicable to the tools and equipment used in the agricultural industry. While learning to apply basic industrial knowledge and skills (engine mechanics, power systems, welding, and carpentry, among others), students may explore a broad range of topics, including the operation, mechanics, and care of farm tools and machines; the construction and repair of structures integral to farm operations; a study of electricity and power principles; and safety procedures."

Do not let educational experiences slip by because you cannot think where to fit them on the transcript—just add them to a Subject Worksheet and consult the Course Classification System for ideas on where they will fit. Few extra activities will be enough for a complete Carnegie unit by themselves, but once recorded on the Subject Worksheets, they can be counted with other activities in the same subject. Your student is learning daily from all that happens, and there is no reason why informal learning experiences cannot be structured to become credit-earning courses and preparation for life.

Special-Needs Records and Transcripts with Judith Munday

Students with special needs often thrive in a homeschool environment. The individualized attention they receive can help them progress despite learning difficulties. Some special-needs students are able to follow a traditional course of study with a few minor modifications in coursework or testing, while others with more severe disabilities must follow a course of study that has been adapted to their needs.

Because I have little personal experience with special-needs students, I interviewed Judith Munday (M.A., M.Ed.) via email. Judi has been helping homeschooled students with special needs for over 18 years. Here are my questions and Judi's responses:

JPC: If a student has been diagnosed as a special-needs student, should parents include this information with the transcript?

JM: This depends on whether the student will require having his or her special needs met by accommodations in higher education. Such accommodations to meet special needs are legally allowable and required under federal law if the college/school gets ANY federal money (including Pell grants).

It is becoming increasingly common for universities and colleges to have robust student services for students who needed extra support to achieve success in high school. Even standardized tests such as the SAT can be taken with specific accommodations IF the student has met specified requirements. One requirement is that the specific learning disability/special need must be documented by someone with appropriate credentials. Keep in mind that most secondary institutions have a special office to support students who have special needs. Keep in mind that most require appropriate documentation that has been done within three years of admission or testing. Counselors want to ensure the student did not suddenly develop a special need to give him or her a better chance for success in college admissions! :-o Yes, I guess it does happen.

It would be impossible to cite all the variables here, so my advice to parents of college-bound and community-college-bound students is to check each school's website for information about allowable accommodations for testing and services available during the educational years. Parents or students may have to dig a bit within a given website to find information, or they can simply call the college or SAT offices. Contact information can be found at the Princeton Review website, among other places.

JPC: Is it a good idea to identify the specific disability or special need on the transcript or in an admissions interview?

JM: It will have to be identified if the student needs documentation for college admission or special considerations during attendance, though not usually on the transcript. The allowable accommodations are based upon the specific needs. In order to qualify for accommodations, the disabilities must be documented by fully qualified professionals. The more specific the documentation, the more access to appropriate help at college will be available. These accommodations can range from having scribes take down dictated test answers for a student with dysgraphia or it may just mean extra time for testing. Some colleges and test situations have more stringent requirements than others. In every case, however, the parents' word alone will not suffice to identify the student's special need.

JPC: Is a student with special needs required to follow any sort of formal plan for his or her education?

JM: The student who has special needs in the homeschool is not required to have a special educational plan (SEP). However, I still recommend special-needs homeschool students have an SEP. It gives a parent the opportunity to form realistic annual goals, and it outlines a means of accountability and provides a way to assess progress at regular intervals during the year. It can also be the end-of-year standard against which to measure the child's achievement. (This can be really helpful for severely disabled students or those whose level is more vocational or life-skills based.)

JPC: Is an SEP the same as an IEP?

JM: IEP (Individualized Education Plan) is a term reserved for those documents created by public schools for public-school students. It lists services that will be paid for by public education funds earmarked to provide special services. It is not appropriate for homeschoolers to use this term for their own student education plans.

JPC: Who creates the SEP?

JM: Parents can create their own SEP, but for students with severe, diagnosed disabilities, a qualified education consultant can provide an appropriate SEP.

JPC: Should the transcript show that the student has been following an SEP?

JM: Since many special-needs students are not on grade level as they progress into high school, they are not always going to be taking high school difficulty-level coursework. Sometimes, they will not be taking all their courses at the same grade level, for example, taking seventh grade math at the same time as they are taking twelfth grade English. I believe for college-bound homeschooled students, the SEP would represent to a college admissions officer that the parent had made an effort to set responsibly high standards and that they had incorporated educational best practices in teaching the child.

Tip from JPC: If you do wish to note this on a transcript, you could add a brief note to the Basic Information section of the transcript, under the heading Grading Scale. Rather than putting in the usual grading scale information, simply put "See attached Student Education Plan." The Check-Off-style transcript might work particularly well for a special-needs student.

JPC: Are special-needs students required to take the same standardized tests as other students?

JM: HSLDA reminds us that in some states we can use Assessments or Evaluations for year-end assessments instead of standardized tests. These can be a bit fuzzy for documentation and transcripts without some terminal standard, which the SEP can provide. National aptitude exams such as the SAT or ACT can be taken with special accommodations such as extra time or reading/writing help.

JPC: Should a parent inform the public-school system of a special-needs diagnosis or the existence of a SEP?

JM: HSLDA folks I have spoken with recommend that parents not provide the public school with any SEP copies or information nor should parents identify the child as having special needs. There are some counties I have heard of where declarations of special needs can almost trigger Social Service visits—others welcome the information and are supportive. It is certainly safer to use licensed, private consultants for special-needs services.

Judith B. Munday, M.A., M.Ed., Educational Consultant is the author of *Teaching a Child with Special Needs at Home and at School.* You may contact her through her website, www.helpinschool.net.

Special Needs Resource Recommendations from Kathy Kuhl

Kathy Kuhl, author of *Homeschooling Your Struggling Learner*, added an additional question and answer to this topic, and suggested a number of helpful links and resources.

Q. Can I give high school credit to someone with special needs who is performing before grade level?

A. Just as struggling learners, including functionally disabled students, receive credit and graduate from public high schools, so homeschool students who have a documented learning disability may also receive appropriate credit. The student's capacity for learning, as diagnosed by a qualified educational consultant, plus an SEP will help to determine how grant credit. The following resources will provide more information.

- Special education law: wrightslaw.com.
- HSLDA front page for special needs: (www.hslda.org/strugglinglearner)
- The College Board gives accommodations for testing if certain criteria are met. It is wise to begin the process 9-12 months before your student needs to take the SAT (www.collegeboard.org/students-with-disabilities).
- *K&W Guide to College Programs & Services for Students with Learning Disabilities or AD/HD* by Marybeth Kravets and Imy Wax, published by Princeton Review

Additional Thoughts from Kathy

Disclosure on the transcript: When my son applied to NVCC, we did not disclose disabilities on the transcript. We disclosed them at an admissions interview, where we brought current evidence of disability and a list of the accommodations I had been providing.

Timing: You need current test results not only for fall of freshman year, you need them when you apply for extended time and other accommodations on the SAT. So schedule evaluations and psycho-educational testing accordingly: early enough to have reports back to submit to the College Board, late enough to still be valid for the first semester of college.

Gap Year: If the student is thinking of taking a gap year, as my son did, you would want to get a documentation of a disability not in ninth but early in tenth grade, so you do not have to pay for more testing during the gap year.

Mandatory Services: If a student can get in to a college on his or her merits, the school is required by law to provide services.

Testing and Accommodations: Once a student qualifies for accommodations from a college, the college that admits them will provide those accommodations throughout the student's enrollment. That means you do not have to pay for more testing after three years of college.

Finally, you can read about Kathy's experience in getting accommodations for her son at her blog: learndifferently.com/homeschoolers-applying-for-accommodations-on-the-college-board-exams-psat-and-sat.

Kathy Kuhl is author of *Homeschooling Your Struggling Learner* and other resources. Through her work, she equips and encourages parents to help children with learning challenges. She speaks to and consults with parents internationally, combining a wealth of information and insight with practical suggestions, humor, and personal experience. (learndifferently.com)

Part 4

Grades, Credit, and the GPA

For many of us, freedom from traditional classroom busywork such as testing and grading is one of the greatest joys of homeschooling. However, this does not necessarily make it any easier to create a transcript! It can be intimidating to think of translating all your student's wonderful living-book learning, unit studies, life experiences, and volunteer activities into credits and grades by which your student will be judged. We will talk about the nuts and bolts of units, grade point averages, and all the other details a bit later in this section, but first, some tips on how to fairly and ethically grade someone you love.

Grading Realistically and Ethically

It is important to understand the traditional meaning of grades and their place in the college admissions process so that you can grade wisely. Although home educators are a diverse group, the actions of each of us affect the reputation of homeschoolers everywhere. Each time a college admissions counselor encounters a homeschooled student whose performance meets or exceeds the expectations created by the grades on his or her transcript, that counselor is likely to gain a more positive impression of homeschoolers. However if a student presents a straight-A transcript but has abysmal test scores and struggles in the classroom, the impression is much different.

How can you grade accurately, fairly, and reasonably objectively? One way is to begin with the end in mind, as Stephen Covey counsels in *The 7 Habits of Highly Effective People*. You need to understand the purpose of the transcript, know what the admissions counselor is looking for, and be aware of the educator's definition of an "A" student.

Traditional Grading Standards

First, know that grading is a practice based upon a set of traditional assumptions. Colleges are aware of geographic and institutional variables in traditional schools, but there are many things that are relatively comparable. When an admissions counselor looks at a group of transcripts, he can assume that a potential student who presents an "A" average on his or her transcript exhibited a learning capacity that put them at the top of their class. In most cases, an "A" earned by a student from a disadvantaged inner-city school will not mean exactly the same as an "A" from a selective, challenging private school, but the grades usually indicate the student's basic potential as well as his or her class standing. This gives the admissions officer a basis for confident comparison.

Home education presents a different set of variables. Each homeschool is unique—we may use classical education, Charlotte Mason, traditional textbooks, unit studies, unschooling, or other options—but each home and family functions independently, and definitions and comparisons can be subjective. Therefore, to a college administrator, the homeschool transcript can present a puzzle. What are the standards used to determine grades? How are results measured? How objective can a parent be when grading his or her own child? I would like to present a few points for you to consider as you begin preparing the transcript.

What is the Purpose of the Transcript?

The primary purpose of the transcript is to showcase your student and his or her achievements. This is usually done for the purpose of getting into college, so the audience for the transcript is most often a college admissions counselor. The counselor's goal is to select students who will be a good fit for the college. He or she needs, at minimum, to know if the student

- can perform at an academic level comparable to other incoming students;
- is a well-rounded individual;
- will bring valuable personal qualities to the university;
- has a talent in the arts, sports, or a particular academic discipline;
- seems likely, based upon previous school records, to graduate.

It is your job, as the responsible parent who certifies the transcript, to convey this information as carefully and accurately as possible.

What is an A Student?

Many homeschoolers are what a college would consider genuine "A" students due to wide reading and/or excellent study habits. An ideal "A" student may have a rich vocabulary, intellectual curiosity, the ability to write and speak articulately, a comparatively quick grasp of new material, and the ability to connect new information with old and reach logical conclusions. An average "A" student may not display all these characteristics, but many of them will be developing or evident. For students at this level, standardized test results, the admission essay, and letters of recommendation will probably support a high grade point average.

B and C Students

Many homeschooled students work at a subject for as long as it takes to master it and receive an A, even if the amount of time required is significantly longer than average. This can be quite beneficial in the younger grades. However, in the high school years a student who needs a significant amount of extra instruction to grasp a subject or multiple retries to pass a test is likely not what an admissions counselor would consider an "A" student. If a student is graded this way, there may be a significant disparity between grades and test scores, which may cause admissions counselors to question the objectivity of the grades.

If you practice this type of mastery learning and want to award a straight "A" transcript to indicate mastery of each subject, go ahead and do so. It may be wise to keep it for your own records, and create a separate transcript for college admissions. The grades may not be significantly lower when you adjust for time and amount of instruction required, but if they are, you may wish to use the Check-Off Transcript. This allows the admissions counselor to see the subjects you have covered, but the admissions essay and standardized test scores will substitute for a GPA in providing comparable information. If you do not want to create two transcripts, at least be sure to provide, in the Basic Information section of the transcript a grading scale or philosophy statement that accurately portrays the criteria you used to determine grades.

Objectivity = Credibility

Admissions office personnel have had enough experience with helicopter parents (the ones who will not stop hovering) that they understand the depth of a parent's love. They tend to begin by assuming that few parents are able to grade objectively, because they not only want their students to be successful, but they can also be somewhat blinded by affection for their child.

Counselors also realize that most homeschool parents have few or no other students with whom to compare levels of achievement.

And really, is it possible to be objective about someone you love? I know that it is hard. When you are drafting a document that will present your child to the world in the sterile terms of a grade point average, it can be difficult to stay focused on the fact that the transcript is just a snapshot of a student's academic performance during the high school years rather than a commentary on his or her entire life (and your teaching ability). As you work with the transcript, you must do your best to be objective without being unnecessarily harsh. It is a balancing act! High school performance does not necessarily predict future success in life. Even if the student has been less than motivated during the high school years and did not work to his potential, the transcript should reflect actual performance. Even if his grade point average is not what you would like it to be, other factors such as the admissions essay, letters of recommendation, and standardized test scores can help round out the picture of who he really is. On the other hand, performance standards in the public schools are pretty dismal, so be sure you do not establish unrealistic standards for perfection.

Set Reasonable Standards

If there is a subject that you are extremely good at, be sure that you are using realistic standards with your students. I was an English major in college, and it was not until I started teaching online English classes and working with other students that I discovered I had been expecting much higher-level work from my own boys than most students were producing in high school. I had actually skipped high school English and was teaching college-level material to my eighth and tenth graders! My boys did fine, but that was probably because they were readers and we had been working at an advanced level in this subject all along.

Having challenging standards can be a very good thing, but unreasonable standards can lead to discouragement and burnout for both student and parent. They can also lead to lower grades than the student deserves. To avoid this, look at sample written assignments by other students in the same grade (k12.thoughtfullearning.com/resources/studentmodels). This will give you a sense of whether your student is working at grade level, and can help you fairly evaluate his or her work.

Use Simple Credibility Clinchers

The good news is that there are objective ways to measure what your student has learned. I call them "credibility clinchers" because that is what they do. A credibility clincher is an objective measurement of a student's performance as it compares to others in the same grade. It can be a standardized test, a class taught and graded by someone who is not related to the student, or awards and accomplishments achieved outside the homeschool.

Any grade from an outside source—a co-op, community college or other class, or other non-mom source—affirms that the student's level of achievement in a particular subject has been objectively measured. When grades from other sources are similar to the grades for classes taken entirely from home, that helps to lend credibility to the grades you give.

Standardized Tests

Standardized tests are often the easiest way to confirm the credibility of the grades on the transcript, unless your student struggles with extreme text anxiety. For college-bound students, the test path usually begins with the PSAT, plus whatever exams the colleges of your student's choice require for entrance. Requirements often include the SAT, CLT, or ACT, and possibly AP, SAT II, or CLEP exams. Students who are not headed to college may opt to take the same exams or the GED.

I recommend following the college-bound path for most students, not only because it can demonstrate a broader range and greater depth of knowledge but also because if your student later changes his or her mind and wants to go to college, the test scores will be ready to go. In addition, the GED is not particularly well regarded, as it can be seen as a last-chance option for students who have dropped out of school.

Because many colleges grant advanced placement, or even credit, for acceptable AP and CLEP scores, taking those exams may give your student a head start on earning college credits. (You can read more about this in my other book, *Get a Jump Start on College! A Practical Guide for Teens*, available at getajumpstartoncollege.com.) Even if the college you choose does not grant credit for one or more of the exams your student takes, the score can still be a credibility clincher.

When you submit test scores with your student's transcript, you provide information that is easily comparable and obviously objective. It works just as well for unschoolers and relaxed record-keepers as it does for meticulous recorders. Standardized test scores provide a simple, straightforward measurement of knowledge that can validate the entire transcript in the eyes of college admissions officials. Needless to say, I highly recommend them. If your student tends to test badly, you may want to use a community college class or two as credibility clinchers, rather than testing.

Grading and granting credit are often the last things we do as a homeschool parent. Just as you have done throughout your student's school days, do the best you can. If your student has done exceptionally well, do not be afraid to show it on the transcript. If he or she has experienced difficulty, grade honestly, but with love and mercy, and an emphasis on the amount of improvement from the beginning to the end of the school year. If you doubt your ability to grade objectively, ask for help. A more experienced home educator, a support group leader, or even a professional homeschool consultant may be able to help. You will find that it is not nearly as hard as it seems!

How To Grade Written Work

As you prepare to create your student's transcript, you will need to assign grades for each class. I have to confess that I never assigned grades to my students' daily work—I just did not feel that it was useful or necessary. However, I did informal Charlotte Mason style evaluations (see www.amblesideonline.org/ExamThoughts.shtml) throughout the semester that allowed me to confidently assign a semester grade when I filled out their transcript.

In a textbook-based curriculum, it is obvious how to grade simple assignments such as vocabulary worksheets, math problems, or multiple-choice exams, but essays and reports can be more difficult to evaluate. A rubric, or checklist of standards, can make it easier to evaluate written work. A constructive evaluation measures the student's work against an objective standard and assesses where and how the work meets or exceeds the standard, and what needs improvement. It is a good idea to evaluate skills from high to low or most to least important. This means evaluating Content standards (Ideas/Concepts and Organization) first, then Style standards (Voice, Sentence Fluency, and Word Choice), and finally, Mechanics (Conventions and Presentation).

If a student has many significant areas of difficulty, evaluate only the skills that have been specifically taught. Be sure the student knows how to consult a writer's handbook and look at models of similar types of writing for questions of structure, style, or usage. Use the numbered sections in a writer's handbook, along with the rubric, to provide constructive, instructional feedback. Even students who begin the year with difficulty tend to catch up as they progress through various assignments and learn by repeatedly going through the read/think/write/evaluate/revise/evaluate cycle throughout the year.

How to Use a Writer's Handbook for Constructive Evaluations

A good writer's handbook makes it easy to offer specific, constructive feedback. If you have used a handbook such as the Excellence in Literature *Handbook for Writers* (writers-handbook.com) or *Writers INC*, you know that information is categorized into numbered paragraphs. These numbers allow you to direct the student to exactly the instruction he or she needs to fix an error or improve a skill.

For example, if your student is having difficulty with subject/verb agreement, you would look in the table of contents of the *Handbook for Writers* and find that subject/verb agreement appears in section 1.8 on page 242. On the student's paper, note the section number so that the student can visit the handbook, read the paragraph, look at the examples, and see how to correct the error. It is quick and efficient, and best of all, much more helpful than just telling the student to be sure that the subject and verb agree.

How to Evaluate the First Draft

After you do an initial read-through of the student's rough draft, get your writer's handbook and a copy of the rubric and evaluate the two Content skills, Ideas/Concepts and Organization. I realize it may be counter-intuitive for many parents to evaluate only the Content standards, because you will see mechanical errors or style problems in the rough draft. However, until the content and organization of the piece are finalized, there is little point in tweaking word choice or sentence fluency. Working only with content helps keep attention on the first draft priorities of ideas and organization, and avoids the distraction of too much red ink.

How to Evaluate a Final Draft

When you receive a revised draft, read through it quickly to gain an overall impression. Have the changes you discussed in the previous draft been satisfactorily made? Use a fresh copy of the rubric to assess each of the seven skill areas and provide a feedback number or symbol for each characteristic listed.

For each draft, return the student's paper with a filled-out rubric, a brief note highlighting the positive and negative things you noticed about the paper, and handbook section numbers so the student can look up challenging items.

Should You Require More than Two Drafts?

Two drafts—a first and a final—are all I recommend. Writing skills improve with each new assignment, and moving through the assignments in a timely manner ensures that students will not get bogged down and end up missing other helpful readings and assignments.

This section is adapted from *Excellence in Literature* and *Evaluate Writing the Easy Way* by Janice Campbell.

Writing Evaluation Rubric

Name: Assignment:	Date: Evaluator:
Content: Ideas and Concepts _ The essay contains a strong, easily identified thesis. _ Interesting ideas and a compelling perspective hold the reader's attention. _ Relevant anecdotes, appropriate quotes, and specific details support the writer's position and demonstrate understanding of the prompt.	**Content: Organization** _ The structure of the paper enhances the presentation of the thesis and supporting ideas. _ Clear transitions move the reader easily from idea to idea. _ Quotes and textual support are blended smoothly, with correct tenses and formatting.
Style: Voice _ The writer speaks directly to the reader, using an appropriate tone and level of formality. _ The writer's voice is individual and engaging, providing a sense of the writer's personality. _ The writer demonstrates awareness of and respect for the audience and purpose of the writing.	**Mechanics: Conventions** _ Standard writing conventions (spelling, punctuation, capitalization, grammar, usage, paragraphing) are observed. _ Citations are correctly formatted using the MLA standard. _ Mechanical or typographical errors are few; only minor touch-ups needed.
Style: Sentence Fluency _ Sentences flow easily with graceful transitions. _ Sentences have a pleasant, appropriate rhythm and cadence when read aloud. _ Sentence structure is varied, with appropriate use of simple, complex, and compound sentences.	**Mechanics: Presentation** _ Essay is in MLA format: Times-New Roman font, 12 pt., 1" margins. _ Paper header with student, class, instructor, and date included. _ Essay prompt included after header and before title. _ Single space following all terminal punctuation.
Style: Word Choice _ Chosen words clearly convey the intended message. _ The words used are precise, interesting, powerful, engaging, and natural. _ The vocabulary is vivid and varied, though not necessarily exotic.	**Comments and Handbook Lookups**

Rating Scale
5 or + indicates that your essay demonstrated outstanding mastery in this area. 4 indicates that the essay is above average. 3 or = indicates that your essay was average and met assignment expectations in this area. 2 indicates that your essay was below average in this area. 1 or - indicates that you should write down this skill as a goal area for improvement.

— This rubric was excerpted from the Excellence in Literature *Handbook for Writers*.

Grading for Unschoolers and the Chronically Relaxed

I f you are an unschooler or a relaxed homeschooler and do not grade your students, you have several options. You may decide to state your philosophy on the transcript and not provide grades at all; you may use the Check-Off Transcript style without grades or with simple retrospective grades; or you may decide to create a portfolio.

Non-Grading Philosophy

You may use the Basic Information space on the transcript to briefly explain your philosophy. All you need is a brief paragraph. For example: "We at Stagg Creek Family School have chosen a cooperative, rather than competitive, learning paradigm. Our students have learned to do their best at whatever subject they begin, and we award credit when it is apparent that the student has attained mastery of the subject. Therefore, we have found it unnecessary to use letter grades." Place this paragraph, or something similar, in the space provided for the Grading Scale.

Check-Off Transcript

If you are structured enough to create a course list using the Class Profiles and Subject Worksheets, the check-off type of transcript shown in the "Create the Transcript" chapter may suit your learning philosophy. This sample was originally adapted (with permission) from a transcript developed for homeschoolers by Mary Baldwin University. It permits students to simply check off the subjects they have covered, though there is room to include grades if you decide to do so.

The portfolio option

If your course of study was so relaxed that you cannot translate it into a traditional list of courses, you may want to consider a portfolio instead of a transcript. In *Homeschooling for Excellence*, David and Micki Colfax briefly describe the papers they submitted with their homeschooled son's college application. These included a "letter … describing his course work and evaluating his strengths and weaknesses as objectively as possible," a long autobiographical essay by the student, and letters of recommendation from several people who had worked with him. This portfolio, along with outstanding standardized test scores, was apparently adequate, for he was accepted to both Yale and Harvard.

That said, most college admissions departments do not have time to look at portfolios. I worked part-time in an admissions department for a couple of years, and I can attest to the astonishing workload teetering on the desks of many admissions counselors. Each counselor receives hundreds of applications to sift through, and they are quickly sorted into "yes," "no," "maybe," and "I do not even want to look at this" piles. Prospective students who want to end up in the "yes" or "maybe" pile can make the counselor's job a lot easier by condensing all their wonderful experiences into a tidy transcript that can be easily compared to others.

If you really want to go with a portfolio, however, the Colfax's ingredients (above) sound just about right. You may wish to include a sample reading log and/or a list of extracurricular activities. I would suggest compiling the documents into a half-inch three-ring binder with page protectors. Once you have it all together, be sure to provide a table of contents at the front of the binder so the admissions counselor can quickly turn to the pages most important to him or her.

Retrospective Grading

If you have followed a more traditional course of study but have not used grades through the high school years, it is still possible to assign grades if you find your student needs a grade point average. The most objective way to do this is by having the student take AP, CLEP, SAT II, or DSST exams in each of the basic subject areas.

If your student is not college-bound, you can also base grades upon the student's overall performance in a subject, rather than the traditional accumulation of individual test and assignment grades. If you want to provide grades based upon overall performance, rather than traditional Carnegie units, be sure to indicate this in the Basic Information section of the transcript. When you think about the letter grade that best fits, consider the following factors:

- Difficulty of the course material
- Progress demonstrated by the student
- Quality of work completed
- Quality of effort expended
- Citizenship factors such as attitude, neatness, and punctuality

The accuracy of retrospective grading depends largely upon the quality of your memory or your records. If you have difficulty remembering details of a specific class, your teen may be able to help. If you are doing this at the end of high school, you will probably know whether your student is average in math, superior in English, or above average in science, and this knowledge can translate into letter grades:

A = Superior/Outstanding

B = Above Average/Good

C = Average/Satisfactory

D = Below Average/Unsatisfactory

Retrospectively assigned grades can be evaluated for objectivity by considering whether the student's standardized test scores seem to confirm the grade level you have assigned to his work. It is better to issue a transcript as simply a list of subjects as in the Check-Off Transcript, than to issue grades that are not supported by other evidence.

Define a Grading Scale

If you provide grades, your transcript should define what level of performance each letter grade represents. Even if you did not do anything more than the informal evaluations I mentioned earlier, you can usually estimate whether your student's work is superior, average, or below average. The verbal and percentage definitions provided below are just suggestions. You may adjust the percentages to match your local schools or use any other words you would prefer to define your standards for performance.

Assign Quality Points

Once you have decided on the letter grade your student will receive, you need to assign a numerical value (quality points or grade points) to each letter grade. This is quite simple, as you can see in the chart above. However you describe your letter grades, your student will receive four quality points for an "A," three for a "B," two for a "C," and one for a "D," unless the course is an honors or AP (college-equivalent) course.

Grading Scale and Quality Point Suggestions					
Letter Grade	Verbal Definition	Percentage Definition	Quality Points	Honors Points	AP/College Points
A	Superior or Outstanding	92–100%	4	4.5	5
B	Above Average	84–91%	3	3.5	4
C	Satisfactory or Average	76–83%	2	2.5	3
D	Below Average or Needs Improvement	68–75%	1	1.5	2

Assigning Grade Points for Plus or Minus Grades

If you want to use plus and minus grades on the high school transcript, just add 1/3 point for a plus or subtract 1/3 of a point for minus from the standard grade point. You will come up with something like this:

Grade	Plus	Minus
A = 4	A+ = 4.33	A- = 3.67
B = 3	B+ = 3.33	B- = 2.67
C = 2	C+ = 2.33	C- = 1.67
D = 1	D+ = 1.33	D- = .67

Using Pass/Fail Grades

If you are considering using Pass/Fail or Complete/Incomplete grades (something I do not recommend unless you have no other option), there are some special issues to consider. Pass/Fail grading can seem simple, but if you are trying to create a transcript with a grade point average (GPA), be aware that a Pass grade receives no more than one quality point, and sometimes none at all. Since you would usually include the credit awarded for a Pass grade in GPA calculations, a Pass grade can negatively affect the GPA. However, because the attempted credit from a Fail grade is counted in the GPA calculations, but receives zero quality points, a Fail grade will always have a negative impact on the GPA. If you have a student athlete who is hoping for NCAA eligibility, it is best not to use Pass/Fail grading, as NCAA calculates a Pass grade with the same number of quality points as a D grade.

How to Grant Credit

When your student has completed the assignments listed on the Class Profile, it is time to grant credit for the class. Although we speak of granting "credit," the traditional measurement of high school achievement is the Carnegie Unit (colleges award "credits"). When we award a Carnegie Unit, the students' hard work is being acknowledged; they are receiving "credit" for their efforts. I hope that is clear!

A class that lasts for one 16- to 18-week semester is worth a half unit, which would appear on a transcript as 0.5. A two-semester, 32- to 36-week class will earn one unit. Thus, a two-semester class worth one unit would equal 120 to 180 hours of guided study, depending upon your state requirements, if any.

1 Carnegie unit = 1 full-year course

OR 1 unit = 120–180 classroom hours of study (a classroom hour is 50–60 minutes)

OR 50–60 minutes/day x 5 days/week x 36 weeks

Some states specify that one unit or credit must equal at least 120 hours of "guided study," which would include both work done in class and as after class study (homework). If your state homeschool law requires the education you provide to be equivalent to this standard, be sure that the grading scale you specify on your transcript mirrors the wording of the standard.

But What If We Do Not Study by the Clock?

Actually, most homeschoolers do not study by the clock or record the exact minutes spent on each subject. Fortunately, it is unnecessary in most states. There are easier ways to keep track of units earned. Most textbooks are designed to be completed in one school year; therefore, when the assigned portions of a textbook are completed you may grant credit. A general rule of thumb is that if the main teaching portion of the class is work from a textbook, that textbook could be consider "completed" when about 80% of lessons have been done). If the textbook is supplementary to other books assigned on the Class Profile sheet for the course, then the credit can be awarded when the assigned portion and other readings and assignments are completed. Therefore credit can be granted when the readings and assignments outlined on a Class Profile are completed.

1 unit/credit = one completed textbook OR Class Profile

How to Grant Credit for Unit Studies

Most formal unit-study publishers provide a breakdown of exactly how credit may be awarded for completion of the study. For unit studies that have no written guidelines, you may grant credit based upon the number of weeks the student was involved with the study. For example, if a study lasts for twelve weeks of six hours per day of study, that is one-third of the school year,. You would grant 1/3 unit for each subject covered. Many unit studies include history, English, art, and literature, so you would grant 1/3 credit for each of these subjects.

1 unit/credit = 1 year unit study

Tip: What you are certifying by granting credit is that the student has studied a specific body of knowledge, not that he knows all there is to know about the subject.

Granting Credit for Honors Classes

Honors classes usually cover more material at a faster pace than a regular class. For example, students who use the Excellence in Literature program for high school English have the option of reading and writing about nine classic works of literature in the regular class, or 18 books with the honors option. For honors classes, grades can be weighted by half a grade point, reflecting the additional depth, breadth, or difficulty of the course assignments.

Granting Credit for AP, Dual Credit, or College-Equivalent Classes

If you are awarding dual credit (actually, you are granting the high school units, while the college credit is granted by your student's college), remember that you are granting credit for material covered, not time spent. Even though it is called dual credit, your only concern is the high school part of the credit. The college credits you record on the Subject Worksheets will have been awarded by the college where the student is enrolled, and they will appear on his or her college transcript as transfer credit. The Carnegie units you grant will appear on the high school transcript.

In some cases, a college instructor may specify the number of credits to grant for dual-credit students, which simplifies everything. If not, the following guidlines may help. If a student takes a one-semester college class that covers an entire textbook on a subject such as Introduction to Biology you may grant one whole Carnegie unit for the class (just as you would if the student finished a high school textbook) and two semester's worth of weighted grade points. Other classes such as mathematics or foreign language may cover only half a textbook each semester. For these, the student would earn half a Carnegie unit plus weighted grade points for each semester of the class.

Listing Advanced Classes on the Transcript

The way you list these classes on the transcript differs according to which transcript style you choose. The Subject-Order transcript is one of the simplest to use if you have earned a lot of credit by exam or through college classes. You can list each course with its corresponding exam or college class, and award credit appropriately, according to the chart below. You will notice in the Subject-Order transcript sample that:

- English I is an ordinary class, earning 0.5 of a unit and 4 quality points per semester.
- English II is an honors class, earning 0.5 of a unit and 4.5 quality points per semester.
- English III and IV are college-level classes, with a six-credit college-level exam used as a course final. For this, you may award one Carnegie unit with corresponding quality points for every three college credits earned. You can see this option used in the Western Civilization courses listed. The student earned a total of two units and twenty quality points over a period of four semesters for this study. If you do this, count the course as two separate classes, e.g., Western Civilization I in the first year and Western Civilization II in the second.

If you have spent four semesters covering the material, as in the Western Civilization example, it would be reasonable to earn one unit for every two semesters of study or three college credits. The student received college-level quality points for this course because he passed the CLEP exams, which confirmed that his knowledge was equivalent to what he would have learned in a college class. If he had done the same amount of work but had not passed the CLEP exams, he would have been awarded Honors points (half of a quality point extra).

Granting grades and credits can be challenging. Use your best judgment based on the breadth and depth of study, time spent, and advanced credits earned. If a future college wants to tweak your numbers, they will do so.

Principles of Granting Credit for Special Classes			
If your student takes...	Equal to ...	Potential college credit would be ...	You would record on the transcript ...
1-semester college class (example: American History 101) or a home-based class with a college-level exam (CLEP, etc.) as a final exam	2 semesters of high school study	3 college credits	1 Carnegie unit plus weighted grade points
2-semester AP class with AP exam	2 semesters of high school study as outlined by AP requirements	Advanced Placement (some colleges may also award credit)	1 Carnegie unit plus weighted grade points
Class or college-level exam covering 1 semester of college material (example: college algebra)	2 semesters of high school study	3 college credits	.5–1 Carnegie unit plus weighted grade points; check with instructor for guidance
Class or college-level exam covering 2 semesters of college study (any of the 6-credit exams.)	4 semesters of high school study	6 college credits	1-2 Carnegie units plus weighted grade points
Remember: you grant only high school credits (Carnegie units) on your transcript. College credit will appear on the student's college transcript.			
Standardized test scores are maintained on an official test transcript by the test company. The student can request that selected scores be sent to colleges once an application has been filed.			

Calculate a Grade Point Average

Once you have determined grades and assigned credits, it is time to calculate the grade point average (GPA). It is not a complicated process—just add together grade points (also called quality points), and divide by the units earned.

How to Calculate the Semester GPA

There are three basic steps to follow in calculating a grade point average (GPA) for a semester:

1. **Assign quality points** (a numerical value) to each grade you have given for each class.

   - The traditional numbers are: A = 4, B = 3, C = 2, D = 1, F = 0. This is what you will use for most classes.

   - For honors courses (a more challenging course with extra readings and assignments), you may use weighted quality points. Just add a half point to each quality point value, making an A worth 4.5 points; B worth 3.5, and so forth.

   - For dual-credit courses and those for which an AP, CLEP, DSST, or SAT II test is taken and passed, grades would be weighted by a full point. This would make the value of "A" equal to 5, "B" equal to 4, and so forth.

   - NOTE: Some colleges do not accept weighted grade points. Check the admission pages on each college's website before submitting a transcript.

2. **Add together all the quality points** for each class (except physical education, which is not usually included in the calculation of the GPA).

3. **Divide** the total number of grade points by the total number of classes taken.

The result will be the grade point average for the semester. If this seems confusing, just look at the sample on the next page. It sounds more complex than it really is.

Cumulative GPA

Calculating a cumulative GPA is essentially the same operation—there are just more numbers to work with. Just as you did for the semester GPA, add together all the quality points earned thus far, and divide the total by the number of Carnegie units earned.

Example of GPA Calculation

If a student has two A grades (worth four quality points each), two B grades (worth three quality points each), and two C grades (worth two quality points each) in a semester, and wants to calculate a grade point average (GPA), this is how it is done:

Calculate quality points for each letter grade.	Add together all the quality points.	Divide the number of quality points (18) by the number of units earned (6).
2 A's = 4 + 4 = 8		
2 B's = 3 + 3 = 6	8 + 6 + 4 = 18	18 / 6 = 3.0 GPA
2 C's = 2 + 2 = 4		

This example shows the operation with simple numbers, but the process is the same, even if you use plus/minus grades or weighted grades.

Free GPA Calculator

If you would like an easy alternative to calculating your grade point average on a calculator (and I realize that is not very hard!), just visit my website at FreeGPACalc.com. I have posted two calculators there for you to use. The first one calculates the semester grade point average, while the second one calculates the cumulative average.

To use the calculators, just select the letter grades you have provided for each class from the drop-down menu. You may choose a standard or weighted grade for each individual class. When you have selected all the grades for the semester, just click the "calculate" button, and record the average. Now, wasn't that easy?

Part 5

Create the Transcript

Now you know the three main parts of the transcript and you have enough information to get started. You may want to photocopy the reproducible blank form in the back and type in your information, but I strongly recommend following the simple instructions for creating the form on your computer. It is much easier to create the basic form, and fill it in as you go, than to try to fit your information neatly into a photocopied form.

Design Basics

Fonts: Use basic, no-frills fonts such as Times New Roman or Arial Narrow. Save the fancy script fonts for the diploma. Primary information, such as identity and course descriptions should be in at least 10 point type; secondary information, such as the grading scale, can be as small as 8 point if absolutely necessary. Just be sure it is legible. Some fonts are narrower than others, so experiment to see which allows you to attractively squeeze in the most information.

Italics: Do not use an underlined font for anything—it looks dated and unprofessional. Italicize items, such as book titles, that would have been underlined in the pre-computer era.

Bold type: The sparing use of bold type can effectively highlight headings and other significant information.

Paper: Use good-quality cream or light gray paper for official copies of the transcript.

If You Need a Second Page

While the transcript is ideally one page, you may have a lot of information to include. If you are about to run onto a second page, here are some suggestions:

- Copy and paste the first page onto a blank second page, so that the Identity and Basic Information sections will appear on both pages.

- If you are using a transcript format that is categorized by semester, put two years on each page, and stretch the tables to fit the page (click on the edge of the table, hold down the left mouse button, and drag the edge to resize).

- Try changing font sizes and font styles to pull the document back to one page. Arial Narrow is a nice clear font that works well in tight spaces.

Remember: think simple, uncluttered, and professional, rather than fancy or decorative. Just as in a résumé, the focus should be on the information rather than an elaborate format. I have included complete instructions for each format to help you create a professional-looking transcript.

All of the transcripts, as well as the diploma, can be created in Microsoft® Word or any other word-processing program that has the ability to create tables. If you do not have a full-featured word-processing program, I recommend using OpenOffice, a free office suite similar to Microsoft Word (openoffice.org). Another option is Google Docs, which is free and has similar, though fewer, features than you will find in the other two programs.

How to Issue an Official Transcript

When your student needs an "official" copy of his transcript for a college or scholarship application, print a copy on good-quality nonwhite paper (gray or cream resume paper works well) and sign the certification line in blue or black ink. If your student has not yet graduated, label current courses as "IP" (in progress), and make sure the graduation date on the transcript is labeled "Projected Graduation Date." Include the GPA for courses completed, and once the current semester is finished, send a final transcript with all the grades and a final GPA filled in. Fold the transcript in thirds and seal in a business-size envelope. You may also sign across the flap of the envelope to demonstrate that the certified transcript has not been opened or tampered with, though this is not usually necessary. Remember that an official transcript will be

- Signed (certified) by one or both parents;
- Sealed in an envelope sent from the school, not from the student.

Alternatives to Doing It Yourself

If, after you know what to do and how to do it, you still do not want to create a transcript, there may be some alternatives. You may want to:

- Have your student enroll in a community college, then transfer to a four-year university;

- Assign transcript creation to your student as part of a class in Business Documents or Computer Competence;

- Barter with an experienced homeschooler or competent friend for transcript services

- Hire someone else who can do the job. (Give them this book, and they will know just what to do!);

- Use a template from my shop at transcripttemplate.com (coming soon).

You can read more about these options below, but I hope you will feel confident enough to tackle the project. It really is not hard!

Community College/Dual Credit

Some community colleges and even a few four-year universities accept teens as dual-credit students without a transcript. You can enroll your student for a semester or two, then have him or her apply to the four-year university as a transfer student. Some in-state four-year schools will not require a high school transcript if a transferring student has 24 credits or more from a community college.

Our boys started taking community college courses when they were 15-16 years old. We found that the application process was fairly simple, and for our first two boys, no high school transcript was needed for admittance. By the time our third and fourth sons began taking classes, a transcript was needed. All incoming students had to take placement tests in language arts and mathematics, and they are usually taken by appointment on campus. Many homeschoolers have followed the dual-credit route and found it a simple way to work through some high school and college courses at the same time. If you would like to do it, here is a checklist:

- Select a convenient community college
- Pick up a course guide or access it online
- Fill out and mail the application for admission
- Apply for financial aid if your student will attend full-time

- Have student schedule and take required placement tests (usually language arts and math)

- Contact dual-credit counselor (if any) to get approval for course choices

- Register and pay for first semester

- Buy books

- Tell your student to go to class, learn new study habits, pass courses!

- Register student for the next semester

When the student is ready to declare a major, it is time to visit the student services office (it is not always called that, but it is the office that handles registration and enrollment) and change his or her student status from non-curricular to curricular (degree-seeking). If your state's community college rules do not permit students under 18 to declare a major without a GED or high school diploma, you have a couple of options. You can have your student take the GED (a relatively easy exam, especially for a student who has been taking college classes), issue your own diploma, or transfer him to a more flexible school. Private colleges are sometimes more flexible than state schools.

Student-Created Transcript

An *Introduction to Computers* or *Fundamentals of Microsoft Office* class can give your student the opportunity to learn how to create many helpful documents including business letters, a résumé, and even the high school transcript form. You would fill out the form, of course, but creating it would be a good practice project for your student.

Barter Services or Hire Someone

In most city phone directories, under "Administrative Services" or "Secretarial Services," you can find someone to type the transcript for you. Or perhaps someone in your local support group would be willing to do so. Just remember that you must have all the information ready, because the person you hire will not be able to run around looking for missing pieces of information, and they may not even realize when something is missing.

The bottom line is that creating a transcript and diploma is a pretty straightforward process once you understand its purpose, its audience, and the practical basics of grading and granting credit. Whether you do it yourself or get someone else to do it for you, you will end up with a transcript that works.

Transcript Formats and Examples

Finally, you are ready to begin creating the transcript! Here are the samples that will serve as models for you. There is no one right way to create a transcript, so feel free to mix and match elements if you are comfortable doing so. If you do not have a lot of computer experience, just choose the design you like best and closely follow the instructions for creating it. You will be amazed at how easy it really is.

I have included a filled-out sample in this chapter, plus a blank copy of each transcript in the back of the book. Basic instructions for re-creating the designs on your computer are also in this chapter. To keep things simple, I tried to use the most common descriptive terms for various functions, rather than focusing on the terminology of a specific program. The instructions assume that you know how to use the basic functions of a word-processing program. If not, you might want to ask someone else—perhaps your student—for help.

How to Choose a Format

Some colleges request a particular format or method of organization, but for those that do not, you may select the format and organization that best highlights your student's strengths.

- Horizontal: This simple, clean format fits on a single page and is organized by time
- Vertical: A classic format that can be organized by subject or time (semester or year). It is possible to fit everything on one page, but this format also makes it simple to do two years per page.
- Subject-organized: For students who have "majored," or taken a number of extra classes in a specific discipline, a subject-ordered transcript can highlight the breadth and depth of their study. This form also makes it easy to see that core requirements have been met.
- Time-organized (semester or year): This format provides information about the chronological order of the courses, making it possible to see a progression of focus and achievement.
- Check-off: This simple form is quick to use, though it provides less detail than others.

Horizontal Transcript Format

This is my favorite format (an example follows the instructions), and it is designed so that once it is set up, your information can be entered by tabbing from field to field (cell to cell within the table). You will not have to worry at all about alignment and spacing, because the table makes it happen.

Here are general instructions for how to create this design in a word-processing program. If you are an experienced computer user, you can skip most of the detail—just create the tables with the correct number of rows and columns; add your information; and tweak until it looks good. If you are less confident, I hope these instructions will help you learn to work with your word-processing program. Just go through the directions step-by-step, realizing that it can look pretty odd at some stages of development. Just keep going and do not worry, and before you know it, you will have a beautiful transcript.

Tip: To find specific instructions for any function of your word-processing program, just ask online. Open Google® or the search engine of your choice and type the question you need to have answered. Just type the main words, and do not worry about punctuation or capitalization. Be sure to include the program name and current year in your query, like this: "how to make line spacing smaller microsoft word 2023" or "how to merge cells open office 2018" or "how to use footers google docs 2027." Whatever your query, you are likely to find that it has been asked before. You may even find videos demonstrating exactly how to do whatever you need to do.

Create and Set Up the Document

1. From the File menu, select "New" to create a blank document for the transcript.

2. Go back to the File menu and choose "Page Setup." Set all margins to 0.5". Ignore your program if it tells you these are outside the printable area, because they usually are not.

3. Save your document, giving it a descriptive file name such as the student's initials followed by "Transcript."

4. Go to the Table menu and activate "Show Gridlines." (If the menu says "Hide Gridlines." simply click on it so that it says "Show Gridlines" instead.) This will enable you to see all the table lines as you work, but the grid will not print. When you finish creating the transcript, you can hide the gridlines and see what it will look like when it's printed.

Create the Tables

1. Choose "Insert Table" from the Table menu and create a table with 11 columns and 45 rows. Select "Autofit to Contents" and click "OK."

2. Go to the first cell of the second row. Click in it and highlight it and the cell to its right, as well as the 2 cells underneath them, so that you have formed a small square made up of the 4 cells. Go to the Table menu, select "Merge Cells," and type "High School Transcript" in the newly merged cells.

3. Highlight and merge the remaining column in the second and third rows of the table, then type the student's name. Hit return and type the student's date of birth. Select both lines of text and align flush right, as shown in the sample.

4. In the first cell beneath "High School Transcript," type "School:". Next, grab the right border of this cell and drag to the left until you reach "School:" and cannot go any farther. Tab to the next cell and enter the name of the school; then hit return and type the address as shown.

5. Tab to the fourth cell and type "Course Description." Continue tabbing and entering column headings in each cell in this row to match the text in the sample table. Choose Arial 10 point, bold italic for your font style.

6. Next go to the fifth cell under "School." Highlight it and the cell next to it. Go to the Table menu and select "Merge Cells." Type "Basic Information" in the newly merged cell.

7. Click in the cell below "Basic Information" and highlight it, the cell next to it, and all of the cells below them except for the last two. Go to the Table menu and select "Merge Cells."

8. Enter the headings as shown in the newly merged cell under "Basic Information," using Arial 9 point, bold italic. Add and delete headings as necessary to match your needs. When you later enter text under the headings, use Arial 8 point in regular font. If you are organizing by year, rather than semester, you will have space to make

the font size bigger. Try bumping each size up one point at a time until you get a size that works.

9. Click in the last cell in this column and highlight it and the cell next to it. Go to the Table menu and select "Merge Cells." Type "Certifying Signature" in Arial 9 point.

10. Now place cursor next to "School." Go to the Table menu and choose "Split Table," which will divide your table into two parts. Select the top table, and go to "Table AutoFormat" in the Table menu. The first format option should be "(none)." Select this, and your table will have no visible borders, as you see in the sample.

11. Select and drag the right edge of the bottom table to align it with the top table, then size the columns to match the sample you have chosen, beginning with the column at the far right. You will notice that as you size the columns, the words in the header column will stack. This will help fit them to the narrower column. Just do not make the column so narrow that the individual words split into pieces!

12. Select the entire second table and in "Table AutoFormat," choose "(none)," then in the Type menu of the Borders palette, choose the option that shows a border around the edge of the selected area.

13. Select the header row, and in the Type menu of the Borders palette, choose the option that shows an inside horizontal border.

14. Finally, highlight all the remaining cells (the Course Description section) and choose Times New Roman or Arial 8 to 10 point font. You may use the largest font size that keeps the tables all on one page.

15. As always, remember that you may adjust font sizes and styles, borders, and column widths as necessary to make it look good. If you find that you need more than one page to enter all the information, your table may automatically break and flow onto the next page. If not, simply insert a page break and copy and paste the table onto a new page. If you do so, you may wish to add page numbers in the footers to indicate page 1 of 2, page 2 of 2, etc.

Connor Hanes
Date of Birth: 10/24/2061

School:
Stagg Creek High School
1300 Stagg Creek Drive
Ashland, Virginia 23005
888-123-4567
parent@email.com
Admission: 08/2074
Graduation: 12/2077

Create the Transcript

Basic Information

Grading Scale:
A—Superior (4)
B—Good (3)
C—Average (2)
D—Below Average (1)
P—Pass (1)
F—Fail (0)
*—Weighted Points

Unit Standard:
One unit represents 120 hours of guided study per 36-week school year.

Abbreviations:
Credit by Examination (AP) or (CLEP) follows Course Description. Grade assigned is based upon percentile ranking of test results, as well as class work, and weighted grade points are granted.

Dual-Credit Courses:
(JSRCC) follows Course Description. Grade and course descriptions issued by J. Sargeant Reynolds Community College. Only high-school-level credit is recorded on this transcript. Weighted grade points are granted for college courses.

Awards & Achievements:

Course Description	Grade	Units Earned	Quality Points
Fall 2074			
English I: Literature & Composition	A	.5	4
Algebra 1/2	B	.5	3
American History	A	.5	4
Earth Science	A	.5	4
Physical Education: Volleyball	B	.5	0
Choir: Mixed Chorus	A	.5	4
Semester Total		3	19
Fall 2075			
English II: American Literature	A	.5	4
Algebra I	B	.5	3
Western Civilization I	B	.5	4*
Biology I	A	.5	4
Physical Education: Swimming	B	.5	0
CSC 155 Computer Concepts and Applications (JSRCC)	B	1	8*
Semester Total		3.5	23
Fall 2076			
English III: British Literature	A	.5	4
Algebra II	B	.5	3
Western Civilization II	A	.5	5*
Chemistry I	A	.5	4
Physical Education: Football	B	.5	0
Choir: Quartet Arrangements	A	.5	4
Semester Total		3	20
Fall 2077			
English IV: World Literature	A	.5	4
Analysis and Interpretation of Literature (CLEP)	A	1	5*
MTH 166 Pre-Calculus With Trigonometry (JSRCC)	C	1	6*
Government and Politics (CLEP)	A	.5	5*
French I (JSRCC)	B	1	8*
Applied Music: Piano	B	.5	3
Semester Total		4.5	31

Course Description	Grade	Units Earned	Quality Points
Spring 2075			
English I: Literature & Composition	A	.5	4
Algebra 1/2	B	.5	3
American History	A	.5	4
Earth Science	A	.5	4
Physical Education: Softball	A	.5	0
Art History and Appreciation	A	.5	4
Semester Total		3	19
Cumulative Total		6	38
Spring 2076			
English II: American Literature	A	.5	4
Algebra I	B	.5	3
Western Civilization I (CLEP)	A	.5	5*
Biology I	A	.5	4
Physical Education: Soccer	B	.5	0
Choir: Mixed and Men's Chorus	A	.5	4
Semester Total		3	20
Cumulative Total		12.5	81
Spring 2077			
English III: British Literature	A	.5	4
Algebra II	B	.5	3
Western Civilization II (CLEP)	A	.5	5*
Chemistry I	A	.5	4
Physical Education: Horseback Riding	B	.5	0
Applied Music: Individual Vocal Instruction	A	.5	4
Semester Total		3	20
Cumulative Total		18.5	121
Spring 2078			
English IV: World Literature (JSRCC)	A	.5	5
Public Speaking (JSRCC)	B	.5	4*
Government and Politics	A	.5	4
French II (JSRCC)	A	1	5*
Art History	A	1	5*
CSC 202 Comp. Sci. (JSRCC)	B	.5	4*
Semester Total		4	27
Cumulative Total		27	174
Cumulative GPA			4.08

Certification of Official Transcript

Vertical Transcript Formats

The vertical transcripts can be organized by time (semester or year) or by subject. This basic format is created with two simple tables, making it easy to enter information by tabbing between cells. I have provided filled out examples for each type of organization. The first example is partially filled and shows how you would indicate a projected graduation date for students who have not graduated. The second example is completely filled as if the student had graduated. The third example is partially filled out, and shows a variation of the vertical layout with lines. Remember that you may adjust font sizes, the spacing between lines, styles, borders, and column widths as necessary to make everything fit nicely.

Space can be tight in these formats, so you may need more than one page to enter all the information. You could place the Identity and Basic Information on one side of a sheet and the Course Record on the other, or stretch the Course Record table until half of it moves to a second page. If you use two separate pages, rather than two sides of one page, add page numbers to indicate page 1 of 2, page 2 of 2, (1/2 and 2/2) and make sure your student's name appears on both sheets. The insert menu of your word processing program may allow you add page numbers automatically but if not, just type the page numbers in the header or footer space. Here are simple instructions for creating the vertical transcript designs.

Create and Set Up Document

1. From the File menu, select "New" to create a blank document for the transcript.

2. Go back to the File menu and choose "Page Setup." Set all margins to 0.5". Ignore your program if it tells you these are outside the printable area, because they usually are not.

3. Save your document, giving it a descriptive file name such as the student's initials followed by "transcript."

4. Go to the Table menu and activate "Show Gridlines." (If the menu says "Hide Gridlines," simply click on it so that it says "Show Gridlines" instead.) This will enable you to see all the table lines as you work, but the grid will not print. When you finish creating the transcript, you can hide the gridlines and see what it will look like when it is printed.

Create Table I for the Identity Section

1. Choose "Insert Table" from the Table menu and create a table with 4 columns and 6 rows. Select "Autofit to Contents" and click "OK."

2. Highlight ("Select") the first row of the table. Go to the Table menu and select "Merge Cells." Type "High School Transcript" and center it in the merged cell.

3. In the first cell of the second row, type "School:" In the third cell in the second row, type "Student:".

4. Now grab the right border of the table, (i.e., place the cursor on the border until you see two parallel bars with arrows pointing right and left), then click and drag to the right margin and release.

5. Grab the right edge of the cell with "Student" and drag to the right past "Transcript" above, about an inch from the edge of the table. Then grab the left edge of the cell with "Student" and drag to the right until the word "Student" lines up underneath "Transcript" above.

6. Grab the right edge of the cell with "Student" again and drag left until it stops and will not go any further. Select the entire table and format the text to Arial 11 point bold.

7. Select the entire table, and go to "Table AutoFormat" (it may have a different description in your program) in the Table menu. The first format option should be "None." Select this and your table will have no visible borders, as you see in the sample.

8. The Identity Section is now ready for you to enter information. You will type information about the school in column 2, and about the student in column 4.

Create Table II for Basic Information and Course Record

1. With your cursor positioned outside the first table, hit return and insert a new table with 7 columns and 10 rows. Select "Autofit to Contents" and click "OK."

2. Select the entire table and in "Table AutoFormat" select "Classic 1," or a similar format that sets off only the header row and first column.

3. Place cursor in the first cell of the first row and type "Basic Information." Tab across the first row, typing in headings for the format you have chosen. Highlight the entire row and format text to Arial 10 point bold italic.

4. Select and drag the right edge of the table to align it with the first table, then size the columns to match the sample you have chosen, beginning with the column at the far right. You will notice that as you size the columns, the words in the header column

will stack. This will help fit them to the narrower column. Just do not make the column so narrow that the individual words split into pieces.

5. Place cursor in the first column under "Basic Information" and select all cells in the column except for the last one. From the Table menu, choose "Merge Cells."

6. Enter the headings as shown under "Basic Information," using Arial 9 point bold italic. Add or delete headings to fit your needs. When you return later to fill in text under the headings, use Arial 8 point regular.

7. In the last cell of this column, type "Certifying Signature" in Arial 9 point regular. Use the line tool in the drawing palette (you will find this under "Toolbars" in the View menu) to draw a line right above the words. This is where you will sign the completed transcript.

8. Now highlight all the remaining cells (the Course Description section) and choose Times New Roman or Arial 8 to 10 point. You may use the largest font size that keeps the tables all on one page.

There! Now you can fill in all the course information by subject, semester, or year. The table will grow to fit, and you will end up with a very sharp-looking transcript. Wasn't that easy?

Sample: Vertical Transcript Organized by Subject

High School Transcript

School: Walnut Creek High School
1913 Honey Run Road
Walnut Creek, Ohio, 40000
888-123-4567
Admission Date: 1/2033

Student: Sebastian Cabot
Date of Birth: 3/19/2031
1808 Indian Tree Trail
Walnut Creek, Ohio, 40000
Anticipated Graduation Date: 12/2037

Basic Information	Course Description by Subject	Sem. 1	Sem. 2	Units	Quality Pts.
Grading Scale:	*English*				
A—Superior (4)	English I: Introduction to Literature	A	A	1	8
B—Good (3)	English II: Literature & Composition - Honors	A	A	1	9
C—Average (2)	English III: American Literature—SATII	A	A	1	10
D—Below Average (1)	English IV: British Literature —AP	A	A	1	10
P—Pass (0)	Introduction to Journalism	A		.5	4
F—Fail (0)	Creative Writing	IP			
Unit Standard:	*History and Social Studies*				
One unit represents 120 hours	U.S. History - Early Colonization to 1877—CLEP	A		1	5
of guided study per 36-week	American History: 1865 to Present		B	1	3
school year.	U.S. Government and Politics —AP	B		1	4
	Western Civ. I - Ancient Near East to 1648 —CLEP	A	A	1	10
	Western Civ. II - 1648 to Present—CLEP	A	A	1	10
Abbreviations:	European History —AP	A	B	1	9
(AP), (SATII), or (CLEP) follows	Human Geography — (projected AP)	IP			
Course Description if final					
exam was a standardized	*Mathematics*				
knowledge test. For these	Algebra I	B	B	1	3
advanced courses, weighted	Algebra II	C	C	1	4
grade points are granted	Geometry	A	B	1	7
based upon a defined body of					
class work plus test results. An	*Foreign Language*				
unweighted final GPA is also	French I	A	A	1	8
provided.	French II	A	A	1	8
	French Literature —AP	A	B	1	9
	Science				
Dual-Credit Courses:	Biology	B	B	1	6
(PCCC) follows Course Descrip-	Chemistry— PCCC	C	C	1	6
tion for dual-credit courses	Physics— PCCC	B	IP		
taken at Prudence Crandall					
Community College. Course	*Fine and Applied Arts*				
description and grades are	Survey of Art History	A		.5	4
determined by the college,	Fundamentals of Drawing		A	.5	4
and only high-school credit	Watercolor Essentials—VMFA	A		.25	4
is recorded on this transcript.	Early Sacred Music: Jerusalem Temple–Middle Ages	IP			
Weighted grade points are					
granted for dual-credit	*Electives*				
courses.	Entrepreneurship 101: Web Page Design	A	IP	.5	

_____

Certified by

Sample: Vertical Transcript Organized by Semester

High School Transcript

School: Stagg Creek High School
13000 Stagg Creek Drive
Ashland, Virginia 23005
888-123-4567
www.EverydayEducation.com

Student: Connor Hanes Campbell
Date of Birth: 10/24/2001
Gender: Male
Admission Date: 08/2014
Graduation Date: 12/2017

Basic Information	Term	Course Description	Grade	Units Earned	Grade Points	GPA
Grading Scale	Fall 2014	English I: Literature & Composition	A	.5	4	
		Algebra ½	B	.5	3	
A—Superior (4)		American History	A	.5	4	
B—Good (3)		Earth Science	A	.5	4	
C—Average (2)		Physical Education: Volleyball	B	.5	0	
D—Below Average (1)		Choir: Mixed Chorus	A	.5	4	
P—Pass (0)		Semester Total		3	19	3.8
F—Fail (0)						
*—Weighted Points	Spring 2015	English I: Literature & Composition	A	5	4	
		Algebra ½	B	.5	3	
Unit Standard		American History	A	.5	4	
One unit represents 120		Earth Science	A	.5	4	
hours guided study per 36-		Physical Education: Softball	A	.5	0	
week school year.		Art History and Appreciation	A	.5	4	
		Semester Total		3	19	3.8
Abbreviations:		Cumulative Total		6	38	
Credit by Examination	Fall 2015					
(AP) or (CLEP) follows		English II: American Literature	A	5	4	
Course Description. Grade		Algebra I	B	.5	3	
assigned is based upon		Western Civilization I	A	.5	5*	
percentile ranking of test		Biology I	A	.5	4	
results, as well as class		Physical Education: Swimming	B	.5	0	
work, and weighted grade		CSC 155 Computer Concepts and Applications (JSRCC)	B	1	8*	
points are granted.		Semester Total		3	24	4.8
	Spring 2016					
Dual-Credit Courses		English II: American Literature	A	5	4	
(JSRCC) follows Course		Algebra I	B	.5	3	
Description. Grade and		Western Civilization I (CLEP)	A	.5	5*	
course descriptions issued		Biology I	A	.5	4	
by J. Sargeant Reynolds		Physical Education: Soccer	B	.5	0	
Community College. Only		Choir: Mixed and Men's Chorus	A	.5	4	
high school level credit is		Semester Total		3	20	4.0
recorded on this transcript.	Fall 2016	Cumulative Total		12	82	
Weighted grade points are						
granted for college		English III: British Literature	A	5	4	
courses.		Algebra II	B	.5	3	
		Western Civilization II	A	.5	5*	
		Chemistry I	A	.5	4	
Awards/Achievements		Physical Education: Football	B	.5	0	
		Choir: Quartet Arrangements	A	.5	4	
	Spring 2017	Semester Total		3	20	4.0
		English III: British Literature	A	5	4	
		Algebra II	B	.5	3	
		Western Civilization II (CLEP)	A	.5	5*	
		Chemistry I	A	.5	4	
		Physical Education: Horse Riding	B	.5	0	
		Applied Music: Individual Vocal Instruction	A	.5	4	
	Fall 2017	Semester Total		3	20	4.0
		Cumulative Total		18	122	
		English IV: World Literature	A	.5	4	
		Analysis and Interpretation of Literature (CLEP)	A	1	10*	
		MTH 166 Pre-Calculus With Trigonometry (JSRCC)	C	1	6*	
		Western Civilization II (CLEP)	A	.5	5*	
Certifying Signature		PHY 121 Principles of Physics (JSRCC)	B	1	8*	
		Applied Music: Piano	B	.5	4	
		Semester Total	A	4.5	37	4.1
		Cumulative Total		22.5	159	4.08

TIP: If you decide to format the vertical transcript by year rather than by semester, you can increase the type size.

Sample: Vertical Format with Lines

Student:			Grading Scale	Unit standard:	Birthdate: Sex:	Final GPA:
School: Address:				Admission Date (to grade 9): Graduation Date:		

Subject	Year	Course Name	Units	Grade	Notes
English		Literature and Composition			
		American Literature			
		British Literature			
		World Literature			
History/ Social Studies		American History & Government to 1860			
		American History & Government 1860-present			
		Western Civilization			
		Survey of World History			
Math		Algebra I			
		Algebra II			
		Precalculus			
		Trigonometry			
Science		Biology			
		Chemistry			
		History			
		Botany			
Art		Art History and Appreciation			
Music		Chorale			
Foreign Language		Latin I			
		Latin II			
		Latin III			
Phys. Ed.		Swimming and Diving			
		Horse Riding (Western)			
Electives		20th C. Dystopian Literature			
		Intro. to Tolkien, Lewis, and Chesterton			
		Principles of Botanical Illustration			
		Entrepreneurship 101			

Check-Off Transcript Format

This basic transcript model can be helpful if you are in a hurry or you have not kept grade records. One way to use it is to simply check off classes taken, sign the certification line, and you are done. Alternatively, you may write a letter grade in the column under the appropriate year. As with each of the other samples, you may use a different title, list parent names in place of the school name, even change the column headings to customize it as you please.

Directions for the Check-Off Transcript

1. Open a new document and set your margins at 0.5".

2. From the Table menu in your word processor, insert a table, with 30 rows and 7 columns. Set it to "Autofit to Contents" so that you can adjust the column widths to match the sample.

3. Select the entire first row of the table, go to the Table menu, and click on "Merge Cells."

4. Type in "Homeschool Transcript" using Arial font at 18 points and centered.

5. In the second row of the table, merge the first three cells and the second four cells, leaving two cells in which you will type the Identity Information.

6. Type the table headings in 10 or 12 point in row 3 of the table, and the subject list in about 8 point in the first column on the left, as shown in the sample on page 111. You may customize the subject list as you prefer.

7. In the second row from the bottom, merge the first three cells and the second four cells, leaving two cells in which you will type the Basic Information.

8. Select the last row of the table, merge the cells, and type in the certification line.

9. If everything is included and there are blank lines left, use the "Delete Row" function to delete them. If that makes the transcript look short, just drag the edge to make it fit the page; select the course record cells; and in the Table menu, click on "Distribute rows evenly."

Sample: Check-Off Transcript

School						Student

Subject Studied	Year 1	Year 2	Year 3	Year 4	Units	Awards/Notes
English						
American Literature						
British Literature						
World Literature						
Foreign Language						
U.S. History						
Western Civilization						
World History						
Civics / Government						
Algebra						
Geometry						
Calculus						
Trigonometry						
Biology						
Chemistry						
Physics						
Environmental Science						
Old Testament						
New Testament						
Art History						
Studio Art						
Music Theory						
Music History / Appreciation						
Applied Music: Vocal						
Applied Music: Piano						
Psychology: Family Life						
Social Science Elective						
Computer Skills						
Computer Programming						
Web Design						
Graphic Arts						
Physical Education						
Elective						
Elective						

Grading Scale:			Abbreviations:

Certified by:

High School Diploma Format

When your student is ready to graduate, you will probably want to create a diploma. The high school diploma is a ceremonial document, much like a certificate. It acknowledges that a student has completed an assigned course of study that meets the requirements of his or her state's Department of Education. It is sometimes used to prove to a prospective employer that an applicant has completed high school. A transcript demonstrates this as well, but it contains more personal information that is not usually needed for employment. Once a student completes a higher level of education—college, technical school, certification program, etc.—the high school diploma can usually be tucked away in the attic, as the higher credential will be what may be requested at job interviews.

How to Create a High School Diploma

I have provided a sample diploma form, which can be tailored to your liking. The traditional wording is simple, and can be edited, as long as the essential meaning remains intact. To re-create the form on your own computer, just follow these simple steps:

1. Open a new document in your word-processing program.

2. Set the document margins to 0.5". You can usually do this in the Document Set-up menu, which is accessed from the File menu.

3. In the Document Set-up menu, select "Landscape" layout, which is usually an icon showing the paper with the long measurement running horizontally. (Most documents are set up in "Portrait Mode," in which the short measurement is horizontal.)

4. Type in the text shown on the next page (or copy and paste, if you are working from the e-book), substituting appropriate information for filler text. Use a traditional font such as Times New Roman or Garamond.

5. Select each line of text and change the font to the size indicated in the parentheses at the end of each line.

6. Below the last line of text, add the signature lines, about 2" long. Place one at the left margin, and tab forward to place the next one at the right margin.

7. If you want a special font for the first line, you might try an all caps Roman style or a traditional calligraphic style such as Old English, Lucida Blackletter, or Edwardian Script.

8. Select all the text (from the Edit menu) and center it. You will usually do this by clicking on an icon that shows a group of lines centered in a box or by choosing "Center" in an Alignment menu.

9. Look at it, and add spaces between the lines to make the spacing pleasing to the eye.

10. Print it on good quality paper and sign in blue or black ink.

Alternatives to creating the diploma from scratch

If you prefer, you can purchase a physical diploma with a cover at hslda.org. In addition, I will be posting a simple diploma template in my shop, which you will be able to reach at DiplomaTemplate.net.

Text for Diploma

High School Diploma

(large font, sometimes Old English or Roman Caps: 24–36 point)

This certifies that

(small font such as Garamond: 14–18 point)

Student's Name

(largest font on the page: 36–48 point)

has completed a College Preparatory Course of Study at OR

has completed the Course of Study prescribed for High School Graduation

(small font: 14–18 point)

School Name

(medium font: 24–28 point)

and is therefore awarded this Diploma

(small font: 14–18 point)

and is entitled to all the Rights and Privileges appertaining thereunto.

(small font: 14–18 point)

Certified, this [number] day of [month, year] by

(small font: 14–18 point)

Parent Signatures

(handwritten on provided lines)

HIGH SCHOOL DIPLOMA

This certifies that

A. Wonderful Student

has ecompleted a College Preparatory Course of Study at

Name of Homeschool

and is therefore awarded this Diploma

and is entitled to all the Rights and Privileges appertaining thereunto.

Certified this 9th day of June 2030, by

_____

Parent Name

_____

Parent Name

Part 6

References, Resources, and Reproducibles

Glossary

AP – See "Advanced Placement."

Accommodations – Special conditions permitted so that students with a disability will be able to compete fairly.

Advanced Placement – The earned privilege of skipping entry-level college course in favor of more advanced study.

Carnegie unit – This is the name for the kind of credit that is awarded in high school. It equals about 120 hours of guided instruction.

CLEP – College Level Examination Program – A group of standardized tests designed to measure subject-area knowledge for the purpose of granting college credit.

Community College – A two-year college, granting associate's degrees.

Credit – Acknowledgement of a student's completion of a specific course of study. Also see "Carnegie unit."

Credit-by-Exam – College credit earned by taking a standardized test.

DSST – A group of standardized, college-level exams, formerly known as DANTES.

DOE – See "Department of Education."

Department of Education – An office of government dedicated to regulating education.

Diploma – A ceremonial document certifying that the recipient has completed high school.

Dual Credit – Classes taken for both high school and college credit.

GED – General Equivalency Diploma. This exam is often taken by people who have dropped out of high school. It signifies that the student has achieved approximately a tenth-grade competence in basic academic subjects.

GPA – See "Grade Point Average."

Grade Points – See "Quality Points."

Grade Point Average – The total score of a student's quality points, divided by the number of classes taken.

Grading Scale – A description of the standards used to define letter grades.

Graduation – A ceremony marking the completion of high school requirements.

FAFSA – Free Application for Student Aid, found at fafsa.ed.gov.

Financial Aid – Grants, loans, scholarships, and work study obtained from the government and from colleges and used to pay tuition.

HSLDA – Home School Legal Defense Association.

High School Record Notebook – A notebook containing Class Profiles and Subject Worksheets from *Transcripts Made Easy*, as well as other documentation described in the planning section of this book.

Homeschool Law – The group of statutes that define conditions for homeschooling in your state.

Honors – A designation that indicates a deliberately challenging class or course of study.

IEP – Individualized Education Plan created by a public school for a specific public-school student with special needs.

Junior College – See "Community College."

Matriculate – To begin college classes.

Portfolio – An organized collection of student work with the purpose of requesting credit.

Quality Points – The numerical value assigned to letter grades in order to calculate a grade point average. Also known as grade points.

Quarter – An academic grading period of approximately ten weeks.

Reading Log – A record of reading done for academic assignments and for pleasure.

SAT – Scholastic Aptitude Test – An exam administered to high school students, designed to test aptitude for higher-level learning.

SAT II – Subject-area exams for high school students, designed to test knowledge in specific subject areas for the purpose of college admissions and/or advanced placement.

SEP – Student Education Plan, usually for students with special needs.

Secondary School – Grades 9–12.

Semester – An academic grading period of 14–18 weeks, usually half the school year.

Special Need – Any requirement for above-average academic assistance due to a physical or mental disability.

Subject Worksheet – A gathering place for raw information related to each subject studied in high school.

Transcript – A record of subjects studied and grades earned.

Unit – See "Carnegie Unit."

Weighted Grade Points – A grading system in which an extra whole or half grade point is awarded for advanced work.

Resources for Planning and Learning

The market is saturated with materials to help you teach your student, but there are a few simple resources that stand out.

AmblesideOnline.org has a well-organized site with free lesson plans for creating a high school experience using the Charlotte Mason model of schooling.

CirceInstitute.org provides articles and podcasts that support families who are interested in the classical model of education.

Secondary School Course Classification System: nces.ed.gov/pubsearch/pubsinfo.asp?pubid=200

Writing models — You can find writing models in the Excellence in Literature curriculum and *Handbook for Writers*, as well as at k12.thoughtfullearning.com/resources/studentmodels.

Excellence in Literature *Handbook for Writers* is a comprehensive reference for learning how to write and self-evaluate.

Time Management: *The 7 Habits of Highly Effective People*, by Stephen Covey – One of the books that I wish everyone could read before making plans for life. Stephen Covey's principles are extremely helpful.

Time Management from the Inside Out by Julie Morgenstern is also excellent.

Peaceful Planning booklets from my website: peacefulplanning.com

Books for Homeschooling Parents

Charlotte Mason's Original Homeschooling Series—This six-volume set lays out an orderly education philosophy and unique teaching methods that achieve excellent results.

Shop Class as Soulcraft: An Inquiry into the Value of Work by Matthew B. Crawford — A thoughtful exploration of the meaning of work and what it means to be human.

Last Child in the Woods: Saving Our Children From Nature-Deficit Disorder by Richard Louv — The best foundation for the study of science is experience in nature. This book explains why.

Dumbing Us Down by John Taylor Gatto – This brief classic is a reminder of some of the reasons it can be a good idea to homeschool through high school.

Hothouse Transplants by Matt Duffy – Stories of homeschoolers who have graduated and are successful and happy in what they are doing. Can be helpful in calming parental fears.

Things We Wish We'd Known edited by Bill and Diana Waring – Short essays from fifty veteran homeschoolers; helpful in determining priorities and defusing worries.

Why Freshmen Fail and How to Avoid It by Dr. Carol Reynolds

Special Needs

Simply Classical: A Beautiful Education for Any Child by Cheryl Swope

Homeschooling the Struggling Learner by Kathy Kuhl

Teaching a Child with Special Needs at Home and at School by Judith B. Munday

Testing and Miscellaneous Resources

Most of these sites provide practice tests and complete information about the exams as well as online registration and links to other helpful information.

Personality/aptitude assessment: 16personalities.com offers a free online personality test that provides results comparable to a Myers-Briggs Type Indicator. This can be helpful to your student during the process of planning for a major or doing career exploration.

SAT I and II, AP, and CLEP: www.collegeboard.com

ACT: www.act.org

DSST: www.getcollegecredit.com

CLT: www.cltexam.com

College textbooks – For standardized test preparation or review, reference for research papers, designing a scope and sequence for a unit study, or an in-depth overview of a subject, it is hard to beat a college textbook. Both students and parents will find useful information there.

NCAA homeschool guidelines: www.ncaa.org/student-athletes/future/home-school-students

Reproducible Forms

Here are a few forms that can help you keep simple high school records. Please do not feel that you must use them all. Use what you need, and feel free to adapt them to your own situation. You may keep them in perfect tidiness on your computer; you may keep them as a slapdash assortment in a three-ring-binder; or you may just go ahead and write in the book. The forms are yours to use within your family as you see fit, but please do not share them online.

List of forms
- Reading Log
- Activities Log
- Class Profile
- Subject Worksheets
- Blank Transcript Forms

Reading Log

Date	Author	Title	Rating	Comments

Activities Log

Date	Activity	Skills	Tools	Time	Comments

Class Profile

Class: Date:

Description:

Outside Resources/Tutors:

Final Grade/Comments:

Readings	Assignments

Grading:

Subject Worksheet: English

High School Units Required: State   College   Other

Units Earned: Grade 9   Grade 10   Grade 11   Grade 12

College Credits Earned: Total _____ By Exam _____ Class _____

Units	Course / Book	Date	Grade	Test Score	Comments
Includes English composition, literature (American, English, world, comparative, etc.), journalism, creative writing, business writing, poetry etc.					

Subject Worksheet: Mathematics

High School Units Required: State _____ College _____ Other _____

Units Earned: Grade 9 _____ Grade 10 _____ Grade 11 _____ Grade 12 _____

College Credits Earned: Total _____ By Exam _____ Class _____

Units Earned	Course / Book	Date	Grade	Test Score	Comments

Includes Algebra I & II, Geometry, Calculus, Trigonometry, etc. Some math classes such as "Consumer Math" are not college prep, but may be listed. You may use text book titles as course names.

Subject Worksheet: History

High School Units Required: State _____ College _____ Other _____

Units Earned: Grade 9 _____ Grade 10 _____ Grade 11 _____ Grade 12 _____

College Credits Earned: Total _____ By Exam _____ Class _____

Units Earned	Course / Book	Date	Grade	Test Score	Comments
Includes American history (at least one unit required), western civilization, European history, African studies, 20th century conflicts, ancient history, etc.					

Subject Worksheet: Natural Sciences

High School Units Required: State _____ College _____ Other _____

Units Earned: Grade 9 _____ Grade 10 _____ Grade 11 _____ Grade 12 _____

College Credits Earned: Total _____ By Exam _____ Class _____

Units Earned	Course / Book	Date	Grade	Test Score	Comments
Includes biology, chemistry, physics, and life sciences, as well as focused topics such as astronomy, anatomy, geology, ecology, archaeology, etc.					

Subject Worksheet: Social Sciences

High School Units Required: State _____ College _____ Other _____

Units Earned: Grade 9 _____ Grade 10 _____ Grade 11 _____ Grade 12 _____

College Credits Earned: Total _____ By Exam _____ Class _____

Units Earned	Course / Book	Date	Grade	Test Score	Comments
Includes law, cultural studies, linguistics, psychology, geography, sociology, anthropology, social policy, economics, political sciences, research methods, etc.					

Subject Worksheet: Religion and Philosophy

High School Units Required: State _____ College _____ Other _____

Units Earned: Grade 9 _____ Grade 10 _____ Grade 11 _____ Grade 12 _____

College Credits Earned: Total _____ By Exam _____ Class _____

Units Earned	Course / Book	Date	Grade	Test Score	Comments

Includes Old and New Testament studies, worldview studies, comparative religions, introduction to philosophy, ethics, etc.

Subject Worksheet: Foreign Language

High School Units Required: State _____ College _____ Other _____

Units Earned: Grade 9 _____ Grade 10 _____ Grade 11 _____ Grade 12 _____

College Credits Earned: Total _____ By Exam _____ Class _____

Units Earned	Course / Book	Date	Grade	Test Score	Comments

Includes the study of any language other than the native tongue, including American Sign Language. High school foreign language study should include grammar and writing, as well as speaking.

Subject Worksheet: Fine Arts

High School Units Required: State _____ College _____ Other _____

Units Earned: Grade 9 _____ Grade 10 _____ Grade 11 _____ Grade 12 _____

College Credits Earned: Total _____ By Exam _____ Class _____

Units Earned	Course / Book	Date	Grade	Test Score	Comments
Includes art history, art appreciation, music theory, music performance, drama, and applied arts, such as painting, sculpture, photography, and dance performance.					

Subject Worksheet: Practical Arts

High School Units Required: State _____ College _____ Other _____

Units Earned: Grade 9 _____ Grade 10 _____ Grade 11 _____ Grade 12 _____

College Credits Earned: Total _____ By Exam _____ Class _____

Units Earned	Course / Book	Date	Grade	Test Score	Comments
Includes driver education, home economics, sewing, woodworking, auto mechanics, computer skills, office skills and procedures, small engine repair, equine management, etc.					

Subject Worksheet: Health/ Physical Education

High School Units Required: State _____ College _____ Other _____

Units Earned: Grade 9 _____ Grade 10 _____ Grade 11 _____ Grade 12 _____

College Credits Earned: Total _____ By Exam _____ Class _____

Units Earned	Course / Book	Date	Grade	Test Score	Comments
Health includes nutrition, fitness, lifestyle, and basic anatomy. Physical Education includes any fitness activity, such as swimming, skiing, bicycling, weight training, aerobics, yoga, or team sports.					

Subject Worksheet: Electives

High School Units Required: State _____ College _____ Other _____

Units Earned: Grade 9 _____ Grade 10 _____ Grade 11 _____ Grade 12 _____

College Credits Earned: Total _____ By Exam _____ Class _____

Units Earned	Course / Book	Date	Grade	Test Score	Comments

Includes any classes or activities that do not fit into other subject categories, such as public speaking, debate, entrepreneurship, volunteer activities, job-related activities, etc.

Subject Worksheet

High School Units Required: State _____ College _____ Other _____

Units Earned: Grade 9 _____ Grade 10 _____ Grade 11 _____ Grade 12 _____

College Credits Earned: Total _____ By Exam _____ Class _____

Units Earned	Course / Book	Date	Grade	Test Score	Comments

Blank Transcript Forms

I would like to think that I have convinced you that it is not hard to create a transcript on the computer. However, if you want to print paper copies as worksheets, here are blank copies of each of the forms. If you would like a transcript with a vintage touch, you could photocopy one of the forms (use the copier settings to increase its size to fill the page), and type in information with a typewriter. This is not an easy process, but it can work. You will need more than one page if you type it, so there are a couple of things you need to do differently.

1. Include the identity and basic information sections on each page, along with a portion (usually half) of the course record.

2. Number the pages to show both the page number and the total number of pages. This way if the pages get separated the admissions department will know how many there are. The numbers should look like this: 1/3, 2/3, 3/3, and the number should be placed somewhere on the lower edge of the page.

3. Once you have it completed, you may want to consider having someone with computer experience re-create it on the computer.

The blank forms include:

- Horizontal Transcript
- Vertical Transcript (two variations)
- Check-Off Transcript

High School Transcript

School:

Student:

Date of Birth:
Gender:
Admission Date:
Graduation Date:

Basic Information	Term	Course Description	Grade	Units Earned	Grade Points	GPA

Grading Scale:
A—Superior (4)
B—Good (3)
C—Average (2)
D—Below Average (1)
P—Pass (0)
F—Fail (0)
*—Weighted Points

Unit Standard:

Abbreviations:

Awards & Achievements:

Certifying Signature

High School Transcript

School:

Admission:
Graduation:

Basic Information

Course Description	Grade	Units Earned	Grade Points

Course Description	Grade	Units Earned	Grade Points

Certification of Official Transcript

High School Transcript

School						Student

Subject Studied	Year 1	Year 2	Year 3	Year 4	Credits	Awards/Notes
English						
American Literature						
British Literature						
World Literature						
Latin						
French						
Spanish						
German						
U.S. History						
Western Civilization						
World History						
Civics / Government						
Pre-Algebra						
Algebra						
Geometry						
Calculus						
Trigonometry						
Physical Science						
Biology						
Chemistry						
Physics						
Environmental Science						
Old Testament						
New Testament						
Religion Elective						
Art History						
Studio Art						
Music Theory						
Music History / Appreciation						
Applied Music: Vocal						
Applied Music: Piano						
Applied Music: Instrumental						
Social Sciences						
Psychology: Family Life						
Social Science Elective						
Business Elective						
Computer Skills						
Computer Programming						
Web Design						
Graphic Arts						
Photography						
Physical Education						
Elective						
Elective						

Grading Scale:

Abbreviations:

Certified by:

High School Transcript

Student:					
School:					
Address:					

Final GPA	Date of Birth:
	Sex:

Admission Date (to grade 9):
Graduation Date:

Subject	Year	Course Name	Units Earned	Grade	Notes
English					
History/ Social Studies					
Math					
Science					
Art					
Music					
Foreign Language					
Phys. Ed.					
Electives					

Notes

Contributors

About the Author

J anice Campbell and her husband Donald homeschooled their four sons from preschool into early college using a lifestyle of learning approach influenced by Charlotte Mason and classical education.

A lifelong reader and learner, Janice has been sharing the joy of learning at homeschool conferences since the 1990s. She speaks on making time for things that matter, teaching literature and writing, homeschooling through high school, record keeping and transcripts, and entrepreneurship. Janice is the author of the award-winning Excellence in Literature curriculum for grades 8-12, *Transcripts Made Easy*, *Get a Jump Start on College*, and other resources, and she writes for various homeschooling magazines, as well as online at EverydayEducation.com, Excellence-in-Literature.com, and DoingWhatMatters.com.

College Preparation Tips

Professor Carol Reynolds is the creator of the *Discovering Music: 300 Years of Interaction in Western Music, Arts, History, and Culture*; and other multi-media courses, and author of *Why Freshman Fail and How to Avoid It*. (ProfessorCarol.com)

Special Needs

Judith B. Munday, M.A., M.Ed., Educational Consultant is the author of *Teaching a Child with Special Needs at Home and at School*. You may contact her through her website, www.helpinschool.net.

Kathy Kuhl is author of *Homeschooling Your Struggling Learner* and other resources. Through her work, she equips and encourages parents to help children with learning challenges. She speaks to and consults with parents internationally, combining a wealth of information and insight with practical suggestions, humor, and personal experience. (www.learndifferently.com)

Everyday Education Book List

Here is our book list. You will always find the most current information and instant ordering, as well as e-books and new items, at www.Everyday-Education.com, but this will give you an idea of what is available in 2018.

Excellence in Literature: Reading and Writing though the Classics—Grades 8-12	
English I: *Introduction to Literature*	
English II: *Lit & Composition*	
English III: *American Literature*	
English IV: *British Literature*	
English V: *World Literature*	
—**Complete Curriculum** (1-5 in books or a binder)	
Handbook for Writers (Reference book for high school and college)	
TimeFrame: The Twaddle-Free Timeline	
Model-Based Writing—coming soon.	

1857 McGuffey Readers with Charlotte Mason Instructions	
First Reader	Fourth Reader
Second Reader	Fifth Reader
Third Reader	Sixth Reader

— SAVE. Set of Readers 1, 2, and 3 OR Set of Readers 4, 5, and 6 OR —Set of all six Readers

Peaceful Planning Booklets
12- Year Planner: A DIY Scope and Sequence for Peaceful Planning
K-8 Student Record
High School Student Record
Reading Log: 100 Books You Won't Forget

Other good stuff
Transcripts Made Easy
Get a Jump Start on College
Perfect Reading, Beautiful Handwriting
CursiveLogic Workbook and cursive art workbook practice set
Elegant Essay by Lesha Myers: Teacher's Manual and Student Book
Evaluate Writing the Easy Way
Working it Out: Poetry Analysis and Devotional with George Herbert
The Living Page: Charlotte Mason Notebooking
French-Ruled Composition Notebooks for handwriting practice
Chenier's *Practical Math Dictionary* and *Application Guide*

CPSIA information can be obtained
at www.ICGtesting.com
Printed in the USA
FFHW010732160419
51801880-57189FF